Drilling
for Gold

Drilling
for Gold

How Corporations Can Successfully Market to Small Businesses

JOHN WARRILLOW

Library of Congress Cataloging-in-Publication Data:

Warrillow, John, 1971–
    Drilling for gold : how corporations can successfully market to small businesses / John Warrillow
        p. cm.
    Includes bibliographical references and index.
    ISBN 0-471-12890-2 (cloth : alk. paper)
        1. Industrial marketing.   2. Industrial procurement.   3. Small business.   I. Title.
    HF5415.1263 .W37 2002
    658.8′4—dc21

                                                          2001046564

Printed in the United States of America.

10 9 8 7 6 5 4 3 2 1

To my team at Warrillow & Co.:
Master your craft
Deliver what you promise
Know the small business market
And do unto others as you'd have done unto you

Contents

Introduction

The small business market is the most important on earth.

The majority of our family and friends depend on small businesses for their paychecks. Most of America's economic output is generated by small business. The world's great inventions—from the light bulb to the automobile—are gifts from the mind of an entrepreneur. More college graduates would rather start a business than be the president of the United States.[1]

And for marketers the fruits of B2b™—big business to small business—are just as ripe: the vast majority of companies in the United States are small businesses. The small business market expands as corporate America retracts. When you sell to small business, your profit margins are under less pressure than when you sell to big business, and entrepreneurs have more important things to do than leave you for a few dollars a month.

But for every great challenge worth achieving, a long, hard battle must be fought. The small business market is a slippery prize that easily wriggles from the hand of the most skilled marketer. To master it, you must be humble and wade deep into the murky trenches of entrepreneurship. You must cast a skeptical eye on the reports of overzealous analysts and market promoters and drill deep into the mind of the entrepreneur.

I started Warrillow & Co. in 1997 in order to help Fortune 500 companies get access to the most important market on

---

1. Survey conducted by Harris Interactive, sponsored by Northwestern Mutual, *Generation 2001: The Second Study,* 2001.

earth. Since that time, our firm has had the opportunity to work with some of the world's great business-to-business brands. Through all of our client work, hundreds of focus groups, and thousands of interviews with small business owners and marketers, our company has discovered four fundamental steps marketers must take to successfully capitalize on the small business sector's potential. This book is broken into four chapters corresponding with each of these fundamental steps:

- *Step 1: Forget about the small business market* describes the importance of segmenting the small business market and reveals some of the unique sectors you can target.
- *Step 2: Find an aggregator* explains how to acquire small business customers cost-effectively.
- *Step 3: Speak their language* explains how to communicate with small business owners and describes some pitfalls to avoid in your advertising.
- *Step 4: Find a simulator* describes how to keep small business owners loyal without breaking the bank.

Before we get started, I want to explain how I use the labels *entrepreneur, small business owner,* and *business owner.* For the purposes of this book, I use all three terms to refer to an individual running a company with fewer than 50 employees. Great debate surrounds the issue of whether differences exist between so-called entrepreneurs and small business owners. Many see entrepreneurs as risk-taking, growth-oriented go-getters. Others attach less desirable qualities to the word *entrepreneur;* for them, the word conjures up images of sleazy snake oil salesmen. For the purposes of this book, however, I use *entrepreneur, small business owner,* and *business owner* interchangeably in an effort not to bore you by repeating one label. In any case, as we go, you will discover much more appropriate labels for the different segments within the small business market.

My purpose in writing this book is not to be a cheerleader

for the small business market. My guess is that you already believe it is an important market or you would not have picked up this book. Instead, my mission is to give you a new framework for considering the small business market and an action plan for capitalizing on it.

Finally, we have tried to use the most current data possible in all of the research statistics presented. However, one of our main sources for nuts-and-bolts demographic data was the United States Census Bureau, which only updates its information every five years. Given the lead time to getting a book published, some statistics are inevitably more dated than others. If you crave more current small business market research and insights, join our community of Fortune 500 marketers by subscribing to *Warrillow Weekly*. A subscription form for this free weekly e-mail communiqué is available at warrillow.com.

Step #1: Forget about the Small Business Market

The first rule of marketing to small businesses successfully is to forget about the small business market. It doesn't exist.

Think about it: what does a dry cleaner have in common with a photographer, and what does either of them share with a biotech entrepreneur? Very little, yet the United States Census puts them all neatly into a category called *small business owners*.

The problem with calling the small business sector a *market* is that markets traditionally have something that binds them together, a common theme about which all members generally agree. The entire small business market is extremely diverse, so the first thing you need to do is figure out a way to slice and dice this market into chunks that are more homogeneous.

This chapter reveals what segments of the small business market exist and how others have successfully gone about carving it up into manageable slices.

***Forget about the so-called* small business market.**

5

Carving off the Sludge

As a small business marketer, one of your first tasks is to size the market. You need to be careful here. Look at any press release relating to small business and you will see wild estimates about the size of the small business market. A large population of small businesses that make it into those estimates will never buy your product or service. In 1997 (the most recent data available for this writing), the United States Census Bureau calculated 21 million small businesses in the United States. However, a huge population of bottom feeders within that 21 million figure will never buy your product. They form the underbelly of the small business market, made up of get-rich-quick schemers, dreamers, and diet pill pushers. Go to any networking event for so-called business owners and you will find them lurking to take advantage of a new entrepreneur. You can see them advertising on the telephone poles of any major North American city—you can't lose 30 pounds in 30 days and neither can you sell your product to these shysters.

After you carve off the sludge, another layer of small businesses needs to be removed from the 21 million estimate; this layer consists of the shell companies that lawyers fabricate to make sure their wealthy clients pay as few taxes as possible. Then you must get rid of all the dormant companies that have been abandoned for one reason or another. You are then left with the legitimate companies, which probably number considerably less than the number your boss told you to target. Unfortunately, calculating this layer accurately is impossible, but our best guess is that it amounts to somewhere between 10 to 15 percent of the 21 million small businesses in the United States.

Take small business market size estimates with a handful of salt.

Forget about the Foosball

New marketers to the small business segment are always amazed to learn the majority of the market has no employees. It's a surprise because the media have conditioned us to conjure up an image of a small business as a place where attractive young people work from exposed brick lofts and play foosball for inspiration.

The reality is that most small businesses are tiny operations that will never be anything more than a quaint pastime for their proprietors. According to the United States Census Bureau, of the 21 million companies in the United States, 74 percent[1] do not have employees. That means these companies have no need for multiextension phone systems, group benefit plans, office space, or computer servers. So if your definition of small business is companies with 1 to 50 employees, you need to take the 21 million figure and peg it around 5.2 million prospects in your total universe (see Figure 1.1).

Overestimating the small business market is a classic blunder made by even the biggest of companies. I remember a project in which a Fortune 500 credit card company called us in to analyze how they could attain a better response rate on their direct marketing efforts targeted at small business owners. The card being offered was a premium card with a very high credit limit, targeted at established small businesses with 5 to 50 employees. The only way to qualify for the card was to have a spotless personal credit history and a substantial personal net worth, including a house or some other tangible asset on the line. This credit card company had been attempting to acquire new cardholders but were consistently pulling less than one percent response rates on their direct mail. Of those who did respond, fewer than one-third actually qualified for the card. As a result, the company was getting less than a third of a percent response rate and the cost per active card acquired was astronomical.

---

1. Bureau of the Census, *Employer and Non-Employer Businesses, 1997*, Economic Division, Bureau of the Census (Washington, D.C., 1997).

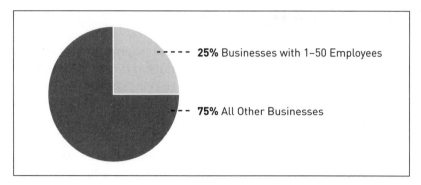

Figure 1.1 Percentage of U.S. Businesses with 1–50 Employees

Source: U.S. Bureau of the Census. *Employer and Non-Employer Businesses*, 1997 Economic Census.

The first thing we did was look at the list of companies targeted. The problem was immediately clear: the marketer had been mailing the entire small business market an offer for a card that less than a quarter of the market could ever use, much less qualify for.

We immediately recommended the company start buying a list of entrepreneurs with 5 to 50 employees instead of the generic small business lists they had been using. This reduced mailing totals by 75 percent. Next, we suggested the company prequalify its target customers' creditworthiness before mailing the offer. Finally, we recommended that the company divert all of the money saved by not mailing the entire small business market to a mailing follow-up via outbound telemarketing to the prospects who might qualify for the card. The result was a considerably lower cost per active cardholder.

Is your target universe really 21 million?

The Great Divide

A world of difference separates a small business owner with employees and one without, a statement that can be illustrated by an experience I had while working on a project for a big phone company. We studied two different sets of focus groups; one was a cluster of small business owners without employees and the other set was composed of business owners with at least five employees. The differences were startling.

The business owners who worked by themselves were generally unsophisticated in business matters. They had more in common with consumers than with other business owners. Their motivation to be entrepreneurs was flexibility and control of their time, their concerns generally centered around their work and a handful of clients, and they marketed their businesses through word of mouth and referrals. Their financial needs were limited to a credit card and a bank account with overdraft protection.

When we then spoke with the business owners with five or more employees, the differences became abundantly clear: these business owners were motivated to create a real business operating independently of them. Their stresses reached beyond clients to include finding employees, keeping good people, obtaining office space to house new employees, and so on. Their financial needs were more sophisticated, and most of these individuals used a bank operating line to shelter their employees from fluctuations in the company's cash flow. I could not believe what a difference just a few employees made. These two types of businesses were only slightly different on paper, yet their challenges and needs were worlds apart.

The number of employees a company has is a quick way to judge a company's size. And firm size—although seemingly somewhat simplistic—is still how some of the world's best business-to-business marketers segment. Dell, for example, is one organization that segments its business-to-business marketing by firm size. Given the amount of customer data their direct-sales model gives them, it is somewhat noteworthy that their segmentation is based largely on size of firm. They have eleven business-to-business segments (see Figure 1.2).

Business Segment	Criteria
Relationship Group	
Global	Companies with 18,000 employees or more that have headquarters outside the U.S. and operations in the U.S., or have headquarters in the U.S. and significant operations in other countries.
Enterprise Accounts	Companies in the U.S. with 18,000 or more employees
Large Corporate Accounts	Companies with 3,500 to 18,000 employees
Preferred Accounts Division	Companies with 400 to 3,500 employees
Internet Partner Division	Internet Service Providers, Application Service Providers, and Web-Hosting companies
Healthcare	Hospitals, HMOs, medical provider groups, medical laboratories
Public	
Federal Government	Federal agencies, federal employees and APO/FPO orders
State and Local Government	State, county, and municipal agencies and organizations
Education	Students, faculty, and staff, as well as K-12 and Higher Education institutional purchases
Home and Small Business	
Small Business Center	Companies based in the U.S. with fewer than 400 employees
Consumer (Home and Home Office)	Home users, both professional and recreational

Figure 1.2 Dell's Segmentation Strategy

Source: Don Peppers and Martha Rogers, *One to One B2B: Customer Relationship Strategies for the Real Economy* (New York: Currency, 2001).

In their book, *One to One B2B: Customer Relationship Strategies for the Real Economy,* Don Peppers and Martha Rogers explain why Dell still relies on company size to segment the business-to-business market:

> While it might appear that Dell has simply arranged its account management organization in a tiered fashion to allo-

cate relatively great priority to larger firms, appearances can be deceiving. Dell's sales organization structure is designed to ensure that it can adapt its service to meet the different needs of different types of customers. Dell has resisted the impulse to group accounts by industry, based on its fundamental understanding that IT [information technology] products are, and probably always will be, perceived as commodities. As a result, what most distinguished one company's IT needs from another's is not the industry in which the company competes, but the nature of the company's procurement and IT management function. And with few exceptions (healthcare being the most obvious), these procurement and management processes are almost always directly related to an enterprise's actual size, rather than its industry.[2]

Some small business marketers fool themselves into believing that size doesn't matter. They reach for stories of business owners who work from home and control multinational empires. They say, "Our market is less about size and more about the kinds of business they're in." The existence of employees as a gauge of the business owner's seriousness is not perfect, but in the absence of a more accurate measure it can be the most effective way to determine whether you are dealing with a real business or just a consumer in a small business owner's clothing.
Size matters.

They Almost Always Lie about This

Be careful if you decide to market to small business owners with a certain number of employees. Entrepreneurs consistently lie about how many employees they have.

2. Don Peppers and Martha Rogers, *One to One B2B: Customer Relationship Strategies for the Real Economy* (New York: Currency, 2001), 90–91.

I remember one project in which a client was interested in understanding the differences between employer-based and non–employer-based companies. We decided to do a series of focus groups. Before we invited attendees to join us, we asked them how many employees they had. Business owners without employees were invited to the non–employer-based groups and anyone claiming to have employees went into the employer-based groups.

The first focus group was to be with employer-based companies. Seven people strolled dutifully into the room and sat down to discuss their businesses. I was thrilled to be among such a wide range of people; we had CEOs who ran computer consultancies, law firms, and construction companies.

About an hour into the night I asked them to describe the best advantage of running their own businesses. Three people said it was the ability to control their time. Two others liked not having a boss and two people liked the fact that they worked from home and avoided a commute. I started to become suspicious. Why were all of these so-called business owners working from home and motivated by controlling their time? Did their employees work from their basements? I then asked the group to confirm how many employees they had. Again, just as they had responded the first time, they answered with numbers ranging from two to fifteen. But something interesting happened this time around—they all gave ranges like 3 to 5 or 7 to 15. My suspicions grew: did they have three or five employees? You would think that with so few employees they should know exactly how many they had and would not need to guess.

Then I caught on. I asked them how many of these so-called employees were full-time workers and how many were part-timers they used only when they were busy. All seven attendees revealed that in fact none of them had what are commonly regarded as real full-time employees. They simply subcontracted people when they needed extra help.

Small business owners lie about how many employees they have because working from home still carries a degree of stigmatization. Although entrepreneurship has become increasingly popular and working from home much more common, outsiders still believe that for a business to be considered real or important, it needs to employ people; thus, small business owners lie about it. They conveniently neglect to mention that of all of those employees, most are contractors and part-timers brought in when needed.

Do all small business owners lie about the number of employees? No. Nevertheless, of all the tendencies we see among small business owners, this issue is the most consistently exaggerated.

Ask if they're full-timers.

The Biggest Segmentation Mistake

Even after you narrow down your target to legitimate business owners, you will be left with a group of customers who have very little in common. Even worse is that they don't see themselves as having much in common, either. Any good marketers worth their white boards will solve this issue by segmenting. The mistake most small business marketers make is that they segment attitudinally first. They reason that the market is too diverse; therefore, they need to understand what makes different entrepreneurs tick. Madison Avenue calls this *psychographics,* a method that usually involves a slew of focus groups across the country. The result is a beautiful presentation lumping small business owners into a variety of segments that usually make marketers feel good for a while. Then it hits them: they can't do anything with these profiles. Such profiles make for great cocktail conversation and executive presentations, but they are completely useless. Mapping a set of qualitative attributes back to a company's database is practically impossible. As a result, these profiles rarely get used.

I remember working with one Fortune 500 technology company that had made this mistake. They had tried to segment the small business market into a variety of psychographic profiles based on attitudes toward technology, attitudes toward company growth, and preferred computer retailers. They had spent hundreds of thousands of dollars with one of the United States' biggest attitudinal research companies. They established names for each of the profiles and presented them at the most senior levels of the organization.

The problem was that boardroom presentations were about the only use for these profiles. It became clear that although these categories were rich and accurate, mapping them back to their own database or against a prospect base was impossible. As a result, the profiles were scrapped.

The other reason building your segmentation in the small business market around behavior is so important is that business owners often have an inflated view of themselves. Some business owners have such a strong vision of what they want their future to be that they start actually visualizing themselves there. They answer questions in a focus group as if their businesses were larger than they actually are. Most of the time they are not intentionally lying or exaggerating; rather, they are simply demonstrating the vision that allowed them to get their businesses off the ground in the first place. If a moderator is unfamiliar with this phenomenon, the result is attitudinal research that captures how entrepreneurs would like to see themselves and not always how they actually are.

Attitudinal profiles are of limited value if you can't find them on a database.

Assessing Value

So before you commission the qualitative research, you must first categorize your small business customers and prospects into groups defined by something that is actionable (i.e., criteria against which one can take action); then do the focus groups. This is an important distinction because as soon as you understand your segments, you will need to communicate with your customer base or a third-party prospect base for the purposes of marketing. The only way to do that is through the use of segments built around data that is available.

How actionable something is comes down to one word—data. If you have good data about the business owners you want to reach, then you'll be able to create actionable tactics. If your data is limited, your segments will be superficial at best, useless at worst.

The best data is historical customer data because it allows you to try to calculate your clients' profitability. Simply put, if you take the revenue you generate from a customer, subtract the cost of the goods or services you sold them, and then subtract the cost of acquiring and servicing the customer, you will understand how profitable the customer is to you. Throw in an analysis of how recently and how often the customer buys from you, and you can establish a level of profitability. After you establish profitability today, you can attempt to estimate Customer Lifetime Value (CLV), which takes into consideration the theoretical value of a customer over a lifetime. The value of a customer to a business varies greatly from one business to the next. I have seen companies look at a wide range of attributes, including everything from growth potential to a client's willingness to act as a reference.

Entire books have been written on customer value analysis, and more than a few consultants make a nice living helping companies establish customer valuation formulas. For our purposes here, assume your small business customers fall into one of three buckets. Put all of your highly profitable customers in the first bucket, put your marginally profitable customers in the second, and fill the third bucket with customers who have negative profitability (in other words, those who cost you money).

In addition to understanding profitability, you need to assess the potential of each client (see Figure 1.3). Assign high potential to customers who you estimate buy from your competitors much more than they buy from you. Assign customers low potential if you already have most of their purchases in your category. After you establish how profitable your clients are or could be, you can then start analyzing

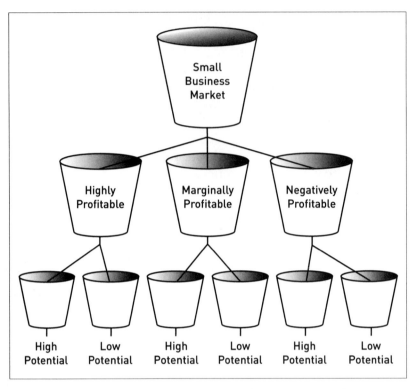

Figure 1.3 Profitability of the Small Business Market

them (qualitatively and in other ways discussed later) and building marketing programs. For profitable customers who give you most of their business, you'll want to think about how to keep them loyal, whereas profitable customers who give someone else most of their business represent good potential, so you need to create an up-sell or cross-sell program.

The behavioral segments help you assess the needs of your clients; profitability and potential help you design a desirable strategy.

In summary, don't make the mistake of segmenting based on attitudinal traits because the segments that you discover will not be very useful. Instead, you should segment based on behavioral attributes that are captured on your database (or a third party's list) first; only then are you ready to figure out what makes your segments tick.

Assign your resources based on potential and value.

Looking for Clues

After you create your segments based on behavior and potential value, you should acquaint yourself with what binds your buckets together. You need to find what all of the companies within a bucket have in common. Knowing what defines your most profitable customers will also help you go out and find more just like them.

Earlier in this section I made some negative comments about how useless attitudinal research profiles are. It is not my intent to discredit attitudinal research. In fact, our company generates a large portion of its revenue by conducting qualitative market research. My suggestion to all small business marketers—and to all of our clients—is to figure out what your profitability buckets are first, then start analyzing the buckets qualitatively.

In addition to doing qualitative research, you can use a number of other ways to analyze your buckets:

- *Demographics of the owner* looks at the owner of the business and includes age, gender, and so on.
- *Firmographics* is a made-up word that business-to-business marketers use when referring to a company's characteristics such as number of employees, growth rate, and revenue.
- *Vertical* refers to the industry in which a small business operates.

The key is not to pick just one method but to use all of the tools at your disposal. In fact, the most successful small business marketers look at their buckets of customers in many ways, constantly trying to find useful similarities.

Use all your tools.

The 98/2 Rule

You've heard of the 80/20 rule. Well, there's a company whose Canadian subsidiary has discovered that a 98/2 rule is a better fit for the small business market. NEBS (New England Business Services) sells business products to the small business market. Unlike many companies that have only recently started talking to entrepreneurs, NEBS has focused on small business since its inception and is a savvy small business marketer to watch.

NEBS Canada understands the importance of looking at the profitability of the small business client. That's why they launched the NEBS Service Plus program as an experiment for the two percent of their customers that are their most profitable. NEBS Service Plus members get special treatment whenever they choose to interact with NEBS. NEBS sends them special catalogs reflecting their status, they get a special toll-free number to call, and their orders are placed in priority and shipped faster than normally. Clearly NEBS could not offer this heightened level of service to its entire customer base, but the company has wisely segmented its small business base and embraced the most important ones.

Did segmenting by profitability pay off for NEBS? Retention levels are up 12 percent as a direct result of the Service Plus Program. Customers have also diversified their purchases by 66 percent and increased the size of their average reorder by 20 percent.

In the small business market, think 98/2, not 80/20.

Dr. Profitable

Knowing which industry presents your best prospects often helps when pinpointing which of your customers are most profitable. Credit card marketer MBNA (Maryland Bank of North America) is a good example. Profitable customers in the credit card business have three characteristics in common: they charge a lot on the card, carry the occasional bal-

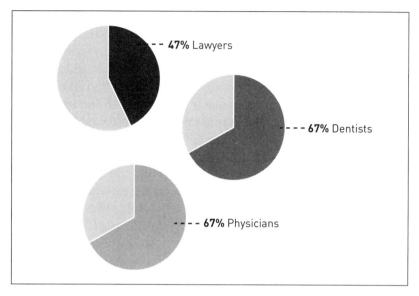

Figure 1.4 Percentage of Target Carrying MBNA Credit Cards
Source: MBNA Annual Report.

ance, and rarely default on their loans. MBNA discovered that this profile happens to be consistent with that of certain professionals such as dentists, lawyers, and doctors.

Well-known for its affinity-marketing prowess, MBNA built cards to appeal to these three vertical markets. They got cozy with the necessary professional organizations and built dominant market share in the incredibly saturated small business credit card market; today, 47 percent of lawyers and 67 percent of all dentists and physicians in the United States carry an MBNA card (see Figure 1.4).

Figure out which industry presents your best prospects.

Weeding out the Wanna-bes

Another strength of segmenting by industry in the small business market is the ability to target real business owners. For every ten small business owners on your database, there are probably a few tire kickers—people who are simply toying with the idea of owning their own business, rather than the actual entrepreneurs you want to reach.

So how can you be sure you're making contact with serious small business owners? One way to approach this question is to think vertically. Dreamers are infatuated with the idea of being a business owner; they go to new entrepreneur meetings and read too many magazine articles about entrepreneurs. People who begin to identify with a certain industry have gotten past the dreaming stage and are actually in business.

I remember a friend of mine named Mark who was one of those guys who always had an idea for what he saw as The Next Big Thing. Every month we'd meet as part of an entrepreneurial association to which we both belonged and each month, Mark would have a new business idea. First he was starting a biotech company that would solve one ailment or another, the next meeting it was a company that designed golf apparel. Sadly, none of these businesses actually got off the ground; they all stayed largely in his head. Mark was in love with the idea of being an entrepreneur. As a result, he couldn't get enough of being around real-life entrepreneurs, reading about them in magazines and trying to associate with them whenever he could.

Real entrepreneurs get past this stage. If they are lucky enough to get beyond start-up, they become hardened and more pragmatic. Their dreams become tempered with a heavy dose of reality; they think less about being entrepreneurs and crave more pragmatic information about succeeding in their industries. In fact, they are less likely to fancy their businesses as *revolutionary* or *unlike any business in history* (common claims from the new entrepreneur) and realize instead that they are part of an industry and that it behooves them to get to know others in it. In other words, business owners that get beyond start-up are often more likely to identify with their industries.

Home Depot does a good job of targeting one industry segment—the company's Services for Contractors program zeroes in on the contractor market and offers a number of services that are available just for them. For example, the program offers a commercial desk that provides assistance solely to contractors, complete with dedicated phone and fax lines to ensure that contractor clients get the information they need right away without having to be passed around from department to department. Finally, a Will Call area allows contractors to call or fax in their order—the Home Depot staff will either deliver the order themselves or help the contractor load it into the vehicle.

By narrowing your focus to a specific industry, you will have a better chance of weeding out the wanna-be entrepreneurs and capturing the attention of the real-life business owner.

Don't invest in dreamers.

How Low Should You Go?

A vertical segmentation strategy is not the most glamorous way to approach the small business market, but it can work.

Industries are classified by a system called North American Industry Classification System (NAICS) codes (formerly SIC or Standard Industrial Classification codes). Each industry falls into a category defined by a series of levels. For instance, let's say you want to go after law firms as a vertical within the small business market. Law offices are found in the two-digit NAICS codes under code 54, "Professional, Scientific and Technical Services." However, if you stop at the two-digit level you also get everything from accounting firms to advertising agencies. Go to a four-digit level and you get "Legal Services," but along with law offices, you get "Title, Abstract and Settlement Offices," too. Not until you go to the five-digit level can you actually zero in on lawyers (see Figure 1.5).

So how low should you go? The key is to understand the NAICS codes and know exactly what you're getting. You need to weigh the benefits of drilling down against the cost and time incurred to do so.

You've got to dig deep to find gold.

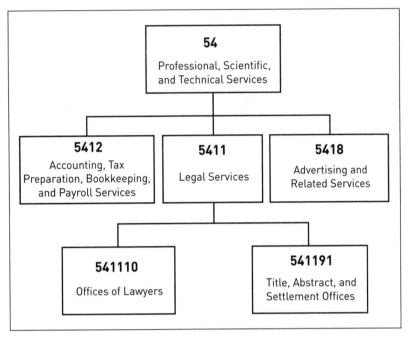

Figure 1.5 Breakdown of NAICS Professional, Scientific, and Technical Services Code

Myth and Reality in the Women's Market

Another way to slice the small business market is to have unique segments based on programs for special interest groups. We've seen this done with young entrepreneurs, Hispanic entrepreneurs, and Afro-American entrepreneurs. One of the most popular segments in this area is the women's entrepreneur market.

A lot has been made of late about the growth in the number of women in the small business market. People cite statistics like *the number of women entrepreneurs is growing at twice the rate as that of men* and *women run over half of all businesses.* These statistics are parroted back in boardrooms all over America, resulting in some major distortions of reality. First, let's start with the facts:

- According to the 1997 United States Census, the number of women-owned businesses grew by 16 percent from 1992 to 1997, while the average growth rate of small businesses was only 6 percent.[3] This means that women-owned businesses are growing at two and one-half times the rate of the small business market in general.

- But a hard look at the Census numbers reveals that the picture is not as clear as it first appears. Of the 5.4 million women-owned businesses in the United States, only 850,000, or 15 percent, are employer-based businesses. In comparison, 30 percent of companies run by men have employees.[4] In other words, men are almost twice as likely to run an employer-based business as women (see Figure 1.6).

- So why is it so important that women-owned businesses tend to be smaller? Because it affects the revenue that they generate and in turn the number of products and services they buy from you. Earlier in this book I described the differences between employer-based and non–employer-based companies. The 1997 Census indicates that nonemployer businesses, which represent 74 percent of all businesses in the United States, only bring in 3 percent of all revenue generated in the United States annually. To reverse this observation, 26 percent of all businesses (those that are employer-based) bring in 97 percent of the revenue generated in the United States.[5]

3. U.S. Bureau of the Census, *Employer and Non-Employer Statistics,* 1997 Economic Census.
4. U.S. Small Business Administration, Office of Advocacy, *Characteristics of Small Business Owners and Employees* (Washington, D.C.: SBA, 1997).
5. U.S. Bureau of the Census, *Employer and Non-Employer Statistics,* 1997 Economic Census.

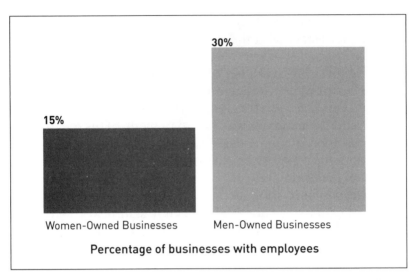

Figure 1.6 Percentage of Employer Businesses by Gender of Business Owner

Source: U.S. Bureau of the Census. *Employer and Non-Employer Businesses*, 1997 Economic Census.

- The sales figures that the Census attributes to women-owned businesses corroborate their findings on non-employer business revenue. Nearly 70 percent of women-owned businesses generate less than $25,000 in annual sales, and only 2 percent bring in more than $1 million annually.
- Flexibility and desire for independence tend to be the major reasons women start a business. According to an NFWBO (National Foundation for Women Business Owners) study, 51 percent of women business owners with prior private-sector experience cite the desire for more flexibility as the major reason for leaving their corporate positions.[6]
- That same study from the NFWBO indicates that

6. Survey conducted by the National Foundation for Women Business Owners (NFWBO), Catalyst and The Committee of 200, sponsored by Salomon Smith Barney, *Paths to Entrepreneurship: New Directions for Women in Business*, February 1998.

women are seven times more likely than men to have turned a personal interest into a business pursuit.[7]

The fact that women's businesses are often smaller than businesses run by men does not mean women are weaker entrepreneurs or somehow inferior. In fact, a strong case can be made that, although women's businesses grow more slowly and tend to be smaller, their businesses are more likely to survive. The point for marketers is that women entrepreneurs are far more likely to get into business for the flexibility it affords them. In North American society, women still shoulder the majority of the child-care responsibilities in a family, a fact that often drives women to seek more flexibility and control over their time.

Socioeconomic discussions aside, the glowing rhetoric surrounding the growth of the women's market often fuels marketers' bad decisions. I can remember being asked to analyze a major bank's media spending against the small business market. This bank had over 300,000 small business customers but made its money on the 10 percent or so with 20 to 99 employees—most of these business owners were men. The other 90 percent of their customer base (the ones with fewer than 20 employees) were only marginally profitable to this bank. Their best small business customers were in traditional businesses like light manufacturing and wholesale distribution because such businesses had large deposits and healthy credit lines that rarely went bad. These industries were also dominated by men.

When we took a look at this bank's media plan, they were pouring almost half of their advertising budget into an all-women's cable network. Their justification was that "women were starting twice as many businesses as men." Not only is an all-women's cable channel untargeted, but also the likelihood of their reaching anyone in their market of 20 to 99 employees in manufacturing and wholesale distribution was slim; what they missed was that, although approximately a quarter of all

7. NFWBO, ibid.

small businesses are run by women, less than 11.4 percent of small companies with 20 to 100 employees are run by women. Additionally, only 12.3 percent of manufacturing firms and 12.1 percent of wholesale distribution firms are run by women. This bank had been duped by one too many misleading reports about the explosive growth of the women's market.

It was a classic example of hype and rhetoric driving bad marketing decisions. So look at your most profitable segments. If you derive most of your profit from smaller companies in the service and retail sectors, a focus on the women's market makes great sense. If not, you may want to find another way to slice the market and avoid a specific emphasis on women.

Temper the hype.

What Women Really Want

I am often asked what makes women entrepreneurs any different from men. Although it is always dangerous to generalize along gender lines, a strong likelihood remains that the women entrepreneurs whom you target are more likely to view their business with what Jim Collins and Jerry Porras refer to as "Pragmatic Idealism." In their book, *Built to Last*, Collins and Porras encourage readers to embrace the "genius of the *and*" instead of the "tyranny of the *or.*" Collins and Porras argue that truly visionary companies embrace the notion that they can have their cake and eat it too. For example, visionary companies believe they can have profits *and* be environmentally responsible, and that two seemingly competing goals do not have to come at the expense of one another.[8]

Women entrepreneurs are more likely to view their companies in a more holistic sense and see their business as playing a larger, more idealistic role than simply producing profits. They often refer to their business and its responsibility as a member of the community.

8. James C. Collins and Jerry I. Porras, *Built to Last: Successful Habits of Visionary Companies* (New York: HarperCollins, 1996).

Seventy-five percent of the women entrepreneurs interviewed for Barbara Thrasher's book, *Smart Women*, claim "Their spiritual philosophy is an integral piece of the foundation on which their business is built."[9] They think about the big picture—how their business is contributing to their community and how their personal values are reflected in their business. These women place a higher emphasis on recruiting employees who share their values. The result, in many cases, is a business with a genuine concern for others.

This insight has implications for you: women entrepreneurs want to do business with companies that share their philosophy, that do their part in the community, that take issues like the environment and child care seriously, and that treat people as people first, not as a line item on a profit and loss (P&L) statement.

So look at your corporation. Is it in touch with its spiritual side? If so, let your customers know.

Women entrepreneurs want to see that you care.

Nightclubs or Golf Clubs?

It's hard to pick up a newspaper or magazine these days without reading about yet another 18-year-old CEO en route to an initial public offering (IPO). It's easy to be lulled into believing that most successful entrepreneurs are under 30 and, considering that getting a young person loyal to a brand early gives them a greater chance of being brand-loyal for life, it seems to make sense to target young entrepreneurs.

It's true that when young entrepreneurs choose a supplier, they are more likely to remain loyal. This stems partly from their lack of time to source new suppliers, but it also has to do with the feeling of having found a partner that extended its hand when they needed it the most. Young entrepreneurs can

9. Barbara L. Thrasher and Madelon A. Smid, *Smart Women: Canadian Entrepreneurs Talk about Making Money, Leadership, Management and Self Development* (MacMillan Canada, 1998), 249.

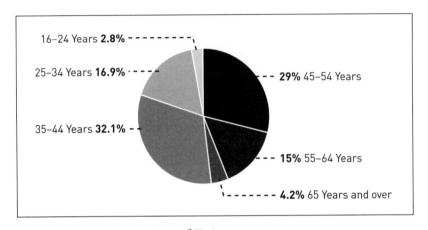

Figure 1.7 Average Age of Entrepreneurs

Source: *NFIB Small Business Policy Guide.* Derived from U.S. Census Bureau, March 1999.

and do become attached to the first suppliers who chose not to ignore them. The next Bill Gates and Richard Branson are in their basements as you read this line.

But before you throw away all of your marketing programs for a hip new image, remember that statistically speaking, less than 3 percent of small business owners in the United States are under 25, whereas almost 50 percent are between 25 and 44 years of age (see Figure 1.7).

Also, in 2000 the median age of the *Inc. 500* CEOs (the annual list of the 500 fastest-growing companies in America) was 40.[10]

What's more, businesses run by 50- to 55-year-old entrepreneurs are more likely to survive than those of small business owners in their twenties—this according to a study done by Warwick Business School's Centre for Small and Medium-Sized Enterprises.[11]

Many of the companies that work with us have the mis-

10. The Inc. 500 Almanac, *Inc. Magazine,* 17 October 2000, 57.

11. Warwick Business School, Centre for Small and Medium Sized Enterprises and Marjolein Peters at EIM for the Forward Studies Unit of the European Commission, *1999–2000 Annual Report—the Economic Impact of Ageing on Start-ups* (Coventry, U.K.: University of Warwick, 2000), 5.

conception that most growing companies are run by twenty-somethings. They choose hip young models for their advertising and try hard to seem relevant. Then they analyze the numbers and realize that the bulk of their profits comes from graying business owners who gravitate toward more realistic, straightforward imagery and messaging. Although betting on the next generation of the small business market makes sense, remember that your quarterly results will come primarily from small business owners who are more concerned about puffy waistlines than Puff Daddy.

Invest in tomorrow, but don't forget about today.

The Asian Majority

Minority-owned businesses are a fast-growing segment of the small business market. According to a United States Small Business Administration report released in 1999,[12] the number of minority-owned firms increased 168 percent from 1987 to 1997. Overall revenue of minority-owned firms grew twice as fast—343 percent—and employment leaped by 362 percent.

But not all minority-owned small businesses are created equal.

From a marketer's perspective, the Asian market represents the most attractive investment in the minority-owned business marketplace. Consider the numbers: although they represented just one-third of all minority-owned businesses, Asian-owned businesses accounted for a majority ($275 billion or 56 percent) of the $495 billion in annual revenue that all minority-owned businesses generated in 1997. Hispanic-owned businesses accounted for 42 percent of minority-owned businesses and 33 percent of the revenue pie. Although Afro-American-owned businesses represented 26 percent of the total, they generated 11 percent of the revenue (see Figure 1.8).

12. U.S. Small Business Administration, Office of Advocacy, *Minorities in Business* (Washington D.C.: SBA, 1999).

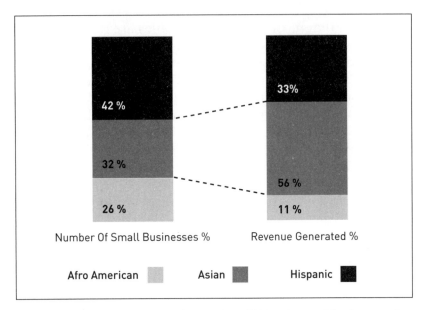

Figure 1.8 Percentage of U.S. Small Business Market and Revenue Generated by Ethnicity of Business Owner

Source: Office of Advocacy of the U.S. Small Business Administration, *Minorities in Business*, Washington, D.C., 1999.

In short, Asian-owned businesses tend to be larger, more successful enterprises than other kinds of minority-owned firms. Asian-owned businesses generated an average of $250,000 in gross revenue, Hispanic-owned firms pulled down $130,000, while the average Afro-American-owned business had an average of $70,000 in annual revenue.

The survival rate of Asian-owned businesses is also significantly higher than that of other minority-owned businesses. Of all the minority-owned firms in operation in 1992, 75.5 percent were still in business in 1996. Asian-owned businesses were more likely to survive, with a full 79.2 percent still going after five years compared to a survival rate of 74.3 percent and 68.9 percent among Hispanic and Afro-American-owned businesses, respectively (see Figure 1.9).

The story continues when you look at the average number of people (not including the owner) employed by minority-

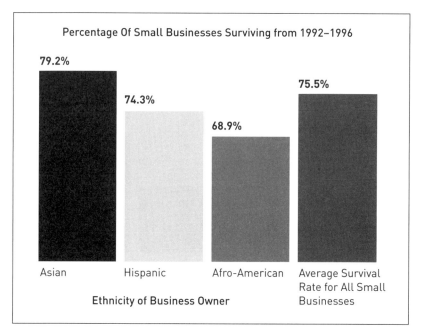

Figure 1.9 Small Business Survival Rates by Ethnicity of Business Owner (1992–1996)

Source: Office of Advocacy of the U.S. Small Business Administration, *Minorities in Business,* Washington, D.C., 1999.

owned firms: for every owner, the average Asian-owned firm employs 1.8 people, whereas the average Hispanic-owned firm has 1.06 employees and the Afro-American-owned firms averaged 0.66 employees (see Figure 1.10).

Finally, when we look at the percentage of all firms employing more than five people, 16.4 percent were Asian-owned businesses, while 13.6 percent were Hispanic-owned and 5.9 percent were Afro-American owned (see Figure 1.11).

All socioeconomic implications of this study aside, the Asian market represents a disproportionately attractive sector for your marketing investment.

Consider a special focus on the Asian entrepreneur market.

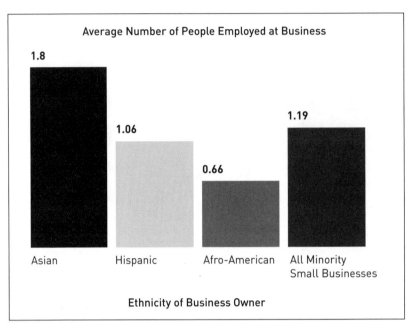

Figure 1.10 Average Number of People Employed by Ethnicity of Business Owner
Source: Office of Advocacy of the U.S. Small Business Administration, *Minorities in Business,* Washington, D.C., 1999.

All in the Family

Another segment of the small business market is family businesses. This segment, although less often used by marketers, is an attractive slice of the market. One reason for its appeal is that family-owned businesses tend to be larger than other businesses. After conducting their *American Family Business Survey* in 1997, Arthur Andersen and MassMutual observed that "many family businesses are big businesses." Indeed, the median annual revenue of respondents was $9 million, a figure suggestive of companies in the 75 to 100 employee range.[13]

13. Arthur Andersen Center for Family Business and MassMutual, *American Family Business Survey,* 1997, 7.

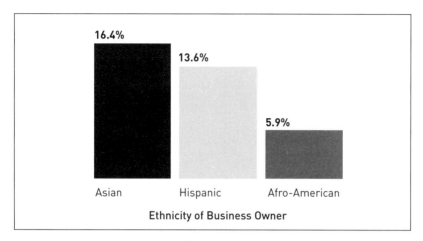

Figure 1.11 Percentage of Minority-Owned Businesses Employing More Than 5 Employees
Source: Office of Advocacy of the U.S. Small Business Administration, *Minorities in Business*, Washington, D.C., 1999.

A survey conducted by Deloitte & Touche also suggests that family-owned businesses skew larger. While three-quarters of all Canadian employer-based businesses fall into the 1 to 9 employee range, only 31 percent of family owned business had 1 to 10 employees, while 26 percent had an impressive 11 to 20 employees and 28 percent boasted 21 to 50 employees (see Figure 1.12).[14]

A family business is defined as "a business that is owned and managed (in the sense of control over the operating decisions) by one or more family members."[15] Central to the definition is the idea that the business is controlled by members of a single (perhaps extended) family.[16]

14. Deloitte & Touche, *Are Canadian Family Businesses an Endangered Species? The First Success Readiness Survey of Canadian Family-Owned Businesses* (University of Waterloo and Deloitte & Touche Centre for Tax Education and Research, 1999), 5.

15. C. E. Aronoff and J. L. Ward, *Family Business Sourcebook* (Detroit: Omnigraphics, 1991).

16. W. C. Handler, "Methodological Issues and Considerations in Studying Family Businesses," *Family Business Review* 2 (1989): 257–276.

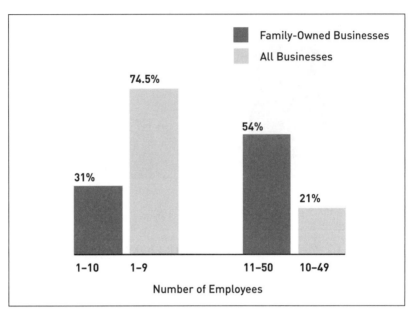

Figure 1.12 Comparison of Family-Owned Businesses and All Canadian Businesses by Employee Size

Source: Deloitte & Touche, *Are Canadian Family Businesses an Endangered Species? The First Success Readiness Survey of Canadian Family-Owned Businesses,* University of Waterloo and Deloitte & Touche Centre for Tax Education and Research, 1999, 5.

Source: Statistics Canada, *County Business Patterns,* June 2000.

These businesses often used to be paternalistic hierarchies defined by tradition and structure. Dad made any decision larger than lunch. The business was passed down to the eldest son to carry on the family's good name. The wives and daughters were put on the payroll for tax purposes and problems were kept in the family.

That's all changing.

According to a 1999 Deloitte & Touche survey, only 33 percent of family businesses think it is important that the business remain in the family.[17] Eighty-one percent of family business owners cite profitability and customer satisfaction as

17. Deloitte & Touche, op. cit., 11.

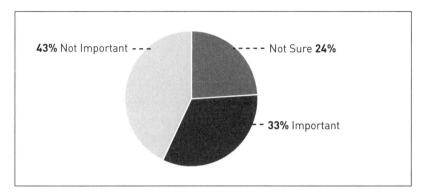

Figure 1.13 Importance to Business Owner of Business Leadership Remaining in the Family
Source: Deloitte & Touche, *Are Canadian Family Businesses an Endangered Species? The First Success Readiness Survey of Canadian Family-Owned Businesses,* University of Waterloo and Deloitte & Touche Centre for Tax Education and Research, 1999, 11.

more important than keeping the family name on the door (see Figure 1.13).

This study goes on to find that 33 percent of family businesses now let outsiders make key decisions with little or no family involvement. Today, a whopping 71 percent of family businesses have outsiders as advisors or on their boards of directors.

Finally, John Messervey, director of the National Family Business Council in Lake Forest, Illinois, observes, "Fathers are gradually becoming more comfortable with the idea that their daughter might be just as good or even better than their son at running the family business. Sons are impatient for succession to occur, while the daughters, in contrast, enjoy sharing responsibility and working with their father."[18]

Targeting family businesses is an interesting approach to segmenting the small business market. They tend to be larger, more successful businesses than the average small business

18. Charlotte Mulhern, "Like Father, Like Daughter: Women Are Running Family Businesses in Record Numbers," *Entrepreneur Magazine,* No. 2 (February 1998).

in the United States. They also have a degree of homogeneity given that family businesses deal with many unique issues like succession and family politics. They have an affinity with their status as a family business, as witnessed by the rise of support groups like the National Family Business Council. But you need to rethink the stereotype of a family business. Most are in the midst of making a transition from traditional family business to a more enlightened contemporary model. It has made some family businesses question everything they've come to count on; for others, change has been a long time coming.

Most of your customers are struggling with succession.

Mountain Climbers, Freedom Fighters, and Craftspeople

Your first step in segmenting the small business market is to look at your customer base behaviorally and divide your customers up into buckets based on how profitable they are to you. Then you need to find the distinguishing characteristics of each bucket, the traits that make each bucket unique. That trait often comes down to what they buy from you, but you may also find that your most profitable buckets have other similarities, including demographics like age, gender, and ethnicity, or firmographics like employee number or industry.

Your next step is to get inside the heads of the entrepreneurs in each of your buckets. Recently we completed an exhaustive attitudinal study in which we conducted 500 in-depth interviews with small business owners, attempting to gain an intimate understanding of their personalities. We found that we could categorize all small business owners into one of three attitudinal profiles. We dubbed them Mountain Climbers, Freedom Fighters, and Craftspeople. Of all 21 million small business owners in the United States, the proportion of Mountain Climbers, Freedom Fighters, and Craftspeople looks like the profile represented by Figure 1.14.

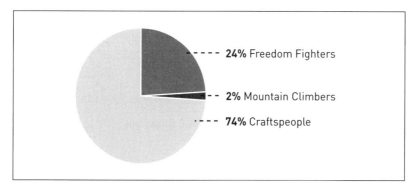

24% Freedom Fighters

2% Mountain Climbers

74% Craftspeople

Figure 1.14 Breakdown of Small Businesses Owners by Psychographic Profile

Each of your customer buckets likely has all three types of entrepreneurs present, but the proportions can change from bucket to bucket.

Mountain Climbers are so named because these entrepreneurs are motivated by growth and achievement. For them, owning a business is all about growing something and achieving something important.

Freedom Fighters, on the other hand, are motivated by independence. To these free spirits who dislike being told what to do, owning a business is the ultimate career choice.

Craftspeople are independent professionals who choose to practice their crafts independently as opposed to working for others.

Know what motivates your small business customer.

Growth Fuel

Although Mountain Climbers are the smallest segment of the market, they are also the group Fortune 500 marketers find most attractive (see Figure 1.15).

Mountain Climbers, motivated by growth and achievement, view entrepreneurship as being about achieving the impossible. They climb mountains in business only to reach the

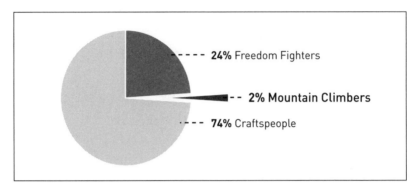

Figure 1.15 Breakdown of Small Businesses Owners by Psychographic Profile

peak and look for the next highest point on the horizon. They're never satisfied. They make up 2 percent of the small business market and typically have between five and fifty employees. Their businesses usually grow at a rate of 20 percent or more.

Mountain Climbers have an interesting relationship with money. They use it as a yardstick to measure their success but are rarely motivated by the money itself. Mountain Climbers are more likely to look at money as growth fuel—the more they have, the faster and farther they can push their businesses. This relationship with money often drives their decisions; they are the most likely to lease equipment, minimizing their monthly payment in an effort to keep as much fuel at their disposal, and they lease office space instead of tying up their cash in a deposit on a building.

I remember interviewing one Mountain Climber who had an incredibly simplistic approach to money. His back-of-a-napkin business plan consisted of trying new ideas until his bank account was empty. Then he would stop expanding and concentrate on the business he already had. As soon as his bank account started looking healthy again, he started experimenting with new ideas. He was like a kid on a Saturday morning, allowance in hand, pedaling as fast as possible to spend every penny at the local candy shop, only to have to wait until next week to get another chance to do it all again.

At one point, this Mountain Climber was considering selling his business but pulled out of the deal at the last minute, fearing that he would "really get himself into trouble" with all of that extra money.

Show Mountain Climbers how to keep their tanks full.

Dr. Kirton Explains

As managers, Mountain Climbers demand a lot. They expect a lot of themselves and, in turn, a lot of their employees. They need very little structure in their lives and, as a result, employees often see them as chaotic and disorganized. One possible explanation can be found in the work of Dr. Michael Kirton. Back in the 1970s, Dr. Kirton set out to understand why some teams of business people are effective while other teams seem dysfunctional.

Kirton's research pointed to a difference in the way people approach problems. Kirton found that when he gave problems for people to solve, some were inclined to look for the answers within the context of what was familiar to them. They drew on personal experience—what they knew—to solve the problems in the most straightforward ways possible. They were fairly quiet in group settings and only spoke up when they were sure their answers were right.

Kirton found that other people were less structured in the way they approached problems. Instead of simply attempting to solve the problem, they tended to look for a way to redefine the question. Their problem-solving techniques were nonlinear and somewhat obscure, drawing on seemingly unrelated facts as they brainstormed. They also demonstrated a different way of interacting with the group, showing a tendency to speak freely without much regard for what they were saying. They offered ideas and waited for the group's reaction. Their feelings didn't get hurt if their idea was not accepted by the group; they would simply propose another idea shortly afterward and wait for the reaction.

Kirton assigned labels to these two different types of

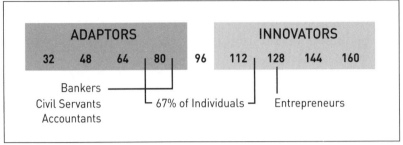

Figure 1.16 Distribution of KAI Scores

Source: Michael J. Kirton, "Adaptors and Innovators: A Description And Measure," *Journal of Applied Psychology* 61(1976): 5, 622–629.

behaviors. He called the first group "Adaptors" and the second group "Innovators."[19] Kirton plotted these different types of people on a continuum with Adaptors on the left and Innovators on the right (see Figure 1.16).

The average score across all professions was 91. He plotted civil servants, engineers, and bank managers on the left, squarely demonstrating "adaptive behaviors" and he plotted marketers and creators on the right. Kirton was careful to emphasize that a high score is not necessarily better or worse; it just represents how an individual approaches problem solving.

Kirton gave entrepreneurs a very high score, plotting them well over to the right on the KAI (Kirton Adaptation-Innovation) continuum.

As prescribed by their typically high KAI score, Mountain Climbers can be difficult employers for more adaptive people. Their operations often seem chaotic, lacking structure and attention to detail. The Mountain Climber, who is only too happy to throw out ideas until something sticks, often dominates meetings. Adaptors often have well-reasoned ideas that never get heard in companies run by Mountain Climbers.

Although Kirton plotted individuals (not corporations) on his continuum, you can be sure that if he rated most Fortune 500 companies, they would be to the far left on the contin-

---

19. Michael J. Kirton, "Adaptors and Innovators: A Description and Measure," *Journal of Applied Psychology* 61 (1976): 5, 622–629.

uum. Almost by definition, large companies need structure and process to exist. In his new book, Kirton explains that large gaps in KAI scores cause difficulty in collaboration and communication.[20]

So as a Fortune 500 company, you're fighting an uphill battle when marketing to Mountain Climbers. They probably already see your company as slow, bureaucratic, and backward. But given their rate of growth and willingness to spend for growth, it's worth trying to change their minds.

No matter how agile your company, Mountain Climbers think you're slow.

The Hardworking Family Man

So what do these Mountain Climbers look like? We did not capture demographics, as our study was strictly based on attitudes. However, an analysis of the Inc. 500 list paints a picture of a hardworking, well-educated family man.[21]

The majority of Mountain Climbers are married (see Figure 1.17).

Over 83 percent have a postsecondary degree (see Figure 1.18).

Most Mountain Climbers are men (see Figure 1.19).

Most are white (see Figure 1.20).

They don't take a lot of time off. The median number of vacation days taken in 1999 was 10.

A few other quick stats:

- Median age of the Inc. 500 CEOs: 40
- Percentage of CEOs who divorced while growing the business: 22.5 percent
- Percentage of CEOs who have received an angel investment: 12 percent

---

20. Michael J. Kirton, *Adaption-Innovation: Cognitive Style in the Context of Managing Change and Diversity* (forthcoming), available at http://www.kaicenter.com/new_book_text.htm.
21. The Inc. 500 Almanac, op. cit.

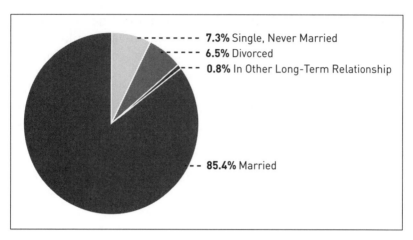

Figure 1.17 Marital Status of the Inc. 500 in the Year 2000
Source: The Inc. 500 Almanac, *Inc. Magazine,* 17 October 2000.

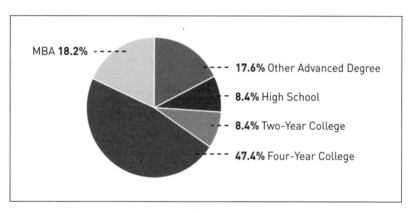

Figure 1.18 Education Level of the Inc. 500 in the Year 2000
Source: The Inc. 500 Almanac, *Inc. Magazine,* 17 October 2000.

- Percentage of CEOs who have made an angel investment in another company: 21 percent

Mountain Climbers work harder than most people you know.

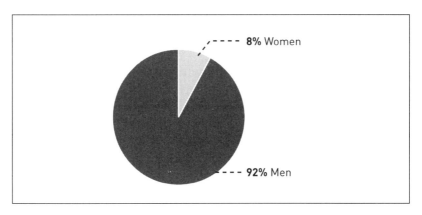

Figure 1.19 Gender of the Inc. 500 in the Year 2000
Source: The Inc. 500 Almanac, *Inc. Magazine*, 17 October 2000.

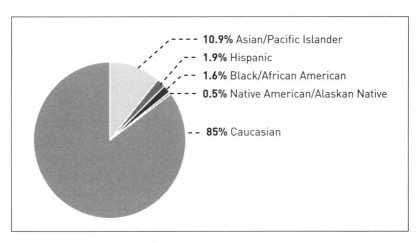

Figure 1.20 Ethnicity of the Inc. 500 in the Year 2000
Source: The Inc. 500 Almanac, *Inc. Magazine*, 17 October 2000.

Chris the Climber

Mountain Climbers are early adopters of technology that can help them grow. They tend to be open to technology that can make their business more nimble and faster on its feet. Mountain Climbers are usually the first small business owners to experiment with new technology. They were the first to carry cell phones in the 80s, laptops in the 90s and BlackBerries in the new millennium.

I remember having lunch with a good friend of mine named Chris. Chris will have Mountain Climber on his gravestone. He is a chronic entrepreneur who started his first business in high school, a guitar repair company that he ran from his basement. When that wasn't enough, he moved on to open a retail store in his home town of St. John's, Newfoundland. He soon tired of that and began plans for a guitar manufacturing company. He spent five years working on a patent to reduce significantly the cost of manufacturing acoustic guitars. Eventually he built a 20,000-square-foot factory to build his guitars and is currently about to remake the acoustic guitar business around the world.

Back to my lunch with Chris. It was around the time when he was working on plans for his guitar manufacturing business. As we sat down, he placed a large, industrial-looking unit on the table—it was his cell phone. This was years before wireless phones became commonplace. During lunch, the cell phone rang three times and each time Chris answered it. I finally asked Chris what he paid to the company that supplied the phone and he rather sheepishly replied that his average airtime bill was around $700 per month.

One might draw the conclusion that Chris was rather rude for taking so many calls during lunch. In fact, Chris is possibly the most courteous person I have ever met—oozing with Newfoundland hospitality and charm—which is why this story is so illustrative of Mountain Climbers. You see, Mountain Climbers are early technology adopters, which is why Chris had one of the first-generation flip phones from Motorola with him that day. They are also the least price-sensitive of the three kinds of entrepreneurs. To him, $700 per month was a good investment to keep in touch with his business.

Mountain Climbers are always looking towards the peak.

Climbing Vertically

Mountain Climbers can be found in practically every industry—dry cleaners who have a vision of creating a national chain and retailers who dream of franchising their concept.

However, as Alexander Russo writes in his report for the National Commission on Entrepreneurship, most Mountain Climbers gravitate toward certain industries: "Growth companies are often clustered around newly deregulated and emerging industry sectors such as telecommunications, financial services and, most obviously, information technology—where potential productivity gains are enormous. This is in stark contrast to the most popular small business sectors such as construction, retailing and cleaning services."[22]

To find Mountain Climbers, choose your vertical.

Mountain Climbers Are Not Inventors

One of the popular myths about entrepreneurship is that successful business owners are inventors. Many envision entrepreneurs toiling away in relative obscurity, working through the night in hopes of building a better mousetrap.

Typically, Mountain Climbers are not inventors with brand-new products; rather, they enjoy rapid growth by tweaking existing business models. Most Mountain Climbers we have interviewed acknowledge that they are improving on an already existing product or service. Most have added a new sales twist, made a refreshing addition to a stale product, or exported a successful concept from one country to another.

You're not targeting the next Einstein.

22. Alexander Russo, Five Myths about Entrepreneurs: Understanding How Businesses Start and Grow, National Commission on Entrepreneurship, Washington, 2001, www.ncoe.org.

The F-Word

Mountain Climbers tend to accept, even embrace failure. They choose to look upon failures as priceless learning experiences, certainly nothing to be embarrassed about. They are able to spin utter disasters into educational experiences.

Charles Schwab had a drive-through animal park and a Music Expo falter before he ventured into discount trading. He chalked these failed businesses up as "priceless learning experiences." Richard Branson's autobiography *Losing My Virginity* describes the failure of his first business—a magazine called *Student*—as the need to "shelve my plans for the time being."[23] Rather than wallow in despair, Branson simply chose to try something new.

A Mountain Climber's ego is an invaluable asset. It is often the armor that protects Mountain Climbers when in intense turmoil. So when a failure threatens their sense of self-worth, they redefine the situation. It's a kind of unconscious defense mechanism that allows them to continue trying when others would have admitted failure and been embarrassed to continue. As a result, Mountain Climbers are the most resilient of the three types of small business owners.

Mountain Climbers don't fail, they learn.

Think Fast

Mountain Climbers tend to make decisions quickly, based on a limited amount of information. Unlike other managers who build a well-documented case to support the wisdom of their decisions against probing superiors, Mountain Climbers tend to act as soon as they are satisfied their decision is the right one.

According to a recent study of 219 growth-oriented entrepreneurs and managers published in the *Journal of Business*

---

23. Richard Branson, *Losing My Virginity* (London: Virgin, 1999),. 79.

46

Venturing: "Entrepreneurs are more likely [than their managerial counterparts] to be overconfident about the correctness of their decisions and more prone to make broad generalizations based on limited experience. While these trends may not seem flattering, they are the attributes that make successful entrepreneurs."[24]

The decision-making process is the subject of hundreds of management books. I won't add to the pile of theories here. Obvious pitfalls accompany this decision-making style, but our purpose is to underscore the implications for you as a marketer trying to reach people who are quick to draw conclusions about the products and services you are selling. Here's a checklist of things to consider for Mountain Climbers who are used to making supplier decisions quickly:

- Headlines: They are important in all communications but doubly so when you are talking to Mountain Climbers. You do not have the time to outline a product benefit in the body copy; they'll never get there. Their decision to turn the page or pitch your direct marketing letter will happen long before reading a benefit in the third line of body copy.
- Signposting: Make effective use of visual signposts in your copy. Use bullets and pull-out quotes and underline liberally so that the skimmer will get the point quickly.
- Word-of-mouth: Nothing speeds up the decision-making process for a Mountain Climber more than a solid endorsement from a respected peer. Get entrepreneurs talking about your product among themselves; it is often all they need to decide on a supplier.

Get to the point.

24. Lowell W. Busenitz and Jay B. Barney, "Differences between Entrepreneurs and Managers in Large Organizations: Biases and Heuristics in Strategic Decision-Making," *Journal of Business Venturing* 12 (1997): 01, 9–30.

The Emotional Paradox of Mountain Climbing

Mountain Climbers tend to ride an emotional roller coaster in their business life, marked by exhilarating highs and punishing lows. I remember talking about entrepreneurship with a Mountain Climber named Grieg Clark. Grieg founded College Pro Painters as a university student and grew it to a $40-million North American operation. When I asked him what he would have done differently if he could do it all over again, he revealed the emotional roller coaster many Mountain Climbers are on: "I'd recommend entrepreneurs try not to ramp up so high on the highs and not crash so low on the lows."

Mountain Climbers invest so much of themselves in their businesses that they derive a disproportionate degree of their self-worth from business achievements. This leaves them on top of the world when things go right but susceptible to mild depression when plans prove unsuccessful. Psychologists have even documented cases of depression among retired Mountain Climbers yearning for an adrenaline fix.

As a marketer targeting Mountain Climbers, remember that you are selling to a person first and foremost. And despite the popular media's best attempts to glamorize them as invincible, that person's real emotions range from paralyzing fear to blissful euphoria.

Mountain Climbers are moody; keep trying until you hit them on a good day.

Go Ahead, Doubt Me

We know that Mountain Climbers are motivated by growth. But where do they get that drive to achieve? Many Mountain Climbers are well-adjusted entrepreneurs who happen to make their living running their own business.

However, for a minority of Mountain Climbers, the drive to grow at all costs is not so healthy. Watch some Mountain

Climbers and every once in a while you will see a deep-seated rage bubbling to the surface. They are probably able to hide it quite well; after all, they have lived with it for a while. Occasionally, however, it boils over and spills out on to the world. This rage is the fuel that drives them faster and harder than anyone else you know.

They are motivated by the desire to prove someone wrong—usually an overly critical parent or a former boss. Dr. Stephen Berglas, management consultant and clinical psychologist from Harvard Medical School, calls it "Entrepreneurial Avenger Syndrome." He describes a patient suffering from it in a recent *Inc. Magazine* article:

> Lenny was driven by a demon that haunts many entrepreneurs: rage at those who dared doubt him. While it helped drive him to succeed, his need to prove others wrong was so powerful that he couldn't begin to control it. Lenny was suffering from a perverse form of revenge-seeking. You might assume that people driven to such overpowering vengefulness would eventually outgrow it, becoming capable of achieving a sense of self-esteem independent of their "I won't get mad, I'll get even" orientation. That is almost never the case.[25]

Berglas goes on to point out the common symptoms of Entrepreneurial Avenger Syndrome include:

- Excessive litigation: suing people for little reason
- A view of the competition as the enemy who must be "beaten"
- Distrust of everyone, resulting in few friends outside of business acquaintances

As a marketer, you need to understand that even well-adjusted Mountain Climbers do not like to be doubted. They

---

25. Steven Berglas, "The Entrepreneurial Avenger," *Inc. Magazine* 20, no. 11 (August 1, 1998). Available at www.inc.com.

bristle at the suggestion they may have to "apply" or be "approved" for anything, so try to avoid this wording on your business forms and processes or get ready for a backlash if a Mountain Climber fails to meet your standards.

Never doubt a Mountain Climber.

Where Mountain Climbers Go Next

Mountain Climbers run growth-oriented companies with up to fifty employees. When a fast-growth company exceeds fifty employees or approximately $5 million in annual revenue, the company gets onto the radar screen of Verne Harnish. Harnish refers to fast-growth companies as "Gazelles" (a term originally coined by David Birch, founder of Cognetics). Verne runs a professional services firm aptly called Gazelles Inc. which specializes in helping fast-growth companies manage and drive their expansion.

Harnish is an influential leader within entrepreneurial circles and has been studying and coaching entrepreneurs for his entire professional life. He co-founded the Association for Collegiate Entrepreneurs (ACE) and founded the Young Entrepreneur Organization (YEO). I wanted to understand from Verne what makes a Gazelle different and how Fortune 500 companies can reach Mountain Climbers when they reach Gazelle status. The following is a transcript from an interview that I conducted with Verne in the summer of 2001:

Q: How do you define Gazelles?

Harnish: Gazelles is a technical term that was defined by David Birch, who owns a company called Cognetics. Birch was a Professor at MIT back in the early eighties. He was the one who studied job growth and was credited with saying that small business has essentially created all the net new jobs as opposed to large companies. But people didn't properly hear him; what he said was that there is only about fifteen percent of what you call small companies that are the true engine of the economy and he labeled them "Gazelles." A Gazelle is any firm that is growing at least twenty percent a year for four years in a row. The ones that are actually generating most of the jobs are the ones between five million and half a billion of revenue. There are two hundred seventeen thousand firms in the U.S. between five million and a half a billion and fifty-six thousand of those are Gazelles.

Q: Given that marketing is all about solving a customer's problem, what are some of the challenges Gazelles face as they grow so quickly?

Harnish: There are three fundamental barriers Gazelles must overcome.

The first is about leadership. As goes the leadership team, so goes the rest of the firm. Whatever strengths or weaknesses exist within the organization can be traced right back to the cohesion of the executive team and their levels of trust, competence, discipline, alignment, and respect. And the two most important attributes of effective leaders are their abilities to predict and delegate. Within the category of prediction we include the ability to set a compelling vision that anticipates market movements. Leaders don't have to be years ahead, just minutes ahead of the market competition, and those they lead. And the ability to accurately predict revenues and earnings is the ultimate test of leadership from the perspective of Wall Street and the public markets.

If we look at the second attribute of effective leadership, the ability to delegate, one can understand why most firms have less than ten employees. Getting others to do something as well as or better than yourself is one of the hardest aspects of leadership, but necessary if you're going to grow the business. Thus most entrepreneurs prefer to operate alone or with a couple of people. To get to the next level of ten employees, the founders at least begin to delegate those functions in which they are weak. As the organization approaches fifty employees, whatever is the strength of the top leader can become the weakness of the organization. From fifty employees up, it's then a matter of adding various layers of mid-level and front-line leaders. The success of the firm is determined by the extent to which the senior leadership team is able to spend time growing the next levels of leadership, which can also predict and delegate effectively.

Successful delegation starts with choosing the right person, keeping in mind the rule that one great person can replace three good people. It's then a four-step process of pinpointing what they are to do, creating a measurement system for monitoring progress, providing feedback, and then giving out appropriately timed recognition and reward.

Q: What's the second barrier Gazelles face as they grow?

Harnish: The second barrier Gazelles are forced to overcome involves systems and structures.

As an organization grows, complexity increases. Take a simple two-point relationship where the two points represent the number of employees, number of product lines, or number of offices within an organization. When you grow fifty percent, represented by adding another point, the interrelationships dramatically increase from two to six or by a factor of three hundred percent. And the complexity increases even more dramatically as you add another point, representing just an additional twenty-five percent growth, jumping from six to twenty-four (calculated by multiplying four times three times two times one). This twenty-five percent growth actually increased complexity by four hundred percent. Therefore, simply doubling from two points to four points increases complexity by a whopping twelve hundred percent.

This increase in complexity leads to stress, miscommunications, increases in costly errors, poor customer service, and greater overall costs. To keep from being buried, an organization must put in place appropriate systems and structures. Going back to the evolution and revolution chart, the first and most basic systems added when jumping from two to ten employees are phone systems and office space. From this point forward, they will always be important considerations as the organization grows. From ten to fifty employees, the accounting system starts to become critical as you struggle to know more precisely if and how which projects, customers, or products are actually making money. From fifty employees or ten million dollars in revenue to fifty million dollars, typically the entire information technology systems need to be upgraded. And above fifty million dollars, you get to revamp them again, as the organization tries to tie all systems to a few if not one common database of customers and employees.

Q: What is the final challenge Gazelles wrestle with?

Harnish: The third and final barrier that Gazelles must tend to is all about market dynamics.

The market makes you look either smart or dumb. When it's going your way, it covers up a lot of mistakes. When fortunes reverse, all your weaknesses seem to be exposed. And there's a counter-intuitive aspect of growing a business, where you have a tendency to focus mostly externally when the firm is under ten million dollars in revenue at a time when just a little more focus internally on establishing healthy organizational habits would pay off in the long run. In turn, as the organization passes ten million dollars, the organizational complexity issues start drawing the attention of the senior team inward at a time when it's probably more important for the team to be focused more externally on the marketplace. This is when it's useful to have outside assistance in dealing with internal issues so you can remain focused externally.

Going back to the evolution and revolution concept and considering the basic measures of a business, those being revenue, gross margin, profit, and cash, there is a sequence of general focus that's important to note. Between start-up and the first million or two in revenue, the key driver is revenue. The focus is on getting interest in the marketplace. As for cash, the entrepreneur has to rely on self-funding or friends and family in the very beginning.

Between one million and ten million dollars, cash concerns are now added to the list as you continue to focus on revenue. Since the organization will typically grow more and faster during this stage than any other, cash will be rapidly consumed. In addition, this is a stage where the organization is experimenting a great deal in order to figure out what its specific focus and position in the market should be. These experiments can be costly.

As the organization passes ten million dollars, internal and external pressures turn up. Externally, the organization is now on more radar screens alerting competitors to its threats. In addition, customers are beginning to demand lower prices as they do more business with a Gazelle. At the same time, internal complexities increase which cause costs to rise faster than revenue. All of this begins to squeeze an organization's gross margins. As the gross margin slips a few points it starves the organization of the extra money it needs to invest in infrastructure like accounting systems and training, creating a snowball effect in the organization as it passes the twenty-five million dollar mark. At this point, it's critical that the company maintain a clear value proposition in the market in order to prevent price erosion, and continually simplify and automate internal processes to reduce costs. Successful organizations can actually see their gross margins increase during this stage of growth.

By fifty million dollars in revenue, an organization is expected to have enough experience and position in the marketplace that it can accurately predict profitability. Not that profit hasn't been important all along as the organization grows. It's just now more critical at this stage that an organization can predict profitability since a few point swings either way represent millions of dollars. Which brings us full circle to the number-one function of a leader, which is the ability to predict. The fundamental journey of a growing business is to create a predictable engine for generating wealth as it creates products and services that satisfy customer needs and creates an environment that attracts top talent.

Growing a business is a dynamic process that requires

a shifting set of priorities as the leadership team navigates the predictable evolutions and revolutions of growth. Continuing to grow the capabilities of leadership throughout the organization; installing systems and structures to manage increasing complexities; and proactively moving with the market dynamics that impact the business are fundamental to successfully growing a business that's fun and profitable.

Q: How can a marketer recognize a Gazelle?

Harnish: You are going to see it physically because the business keeps moving. You're going to tell a Gazelle because of the fact that they are showing up more and more in articles in the newspaper. You're going to start hearing more about them. They are clearly making a move out there in the marketplace.

Q: Can you buy a list of Gazelles?

Harnish: Yes, you can buy a list from Dave Birch at Cognetics. *Inc. Magazine* has a good list of Gazelles in their Inc. 500 list. American Express has their idea of what Gazelles are based on increased purchases on the American Express card. NASDAQ [National Association of Securities Dealers Automated Quotation System] also tracks Gazelles. Another good one is "Cahner's decision maker" database which gives you (selects) like title, employee size and sales volume.

Q: Can you give me an example of a company that has been successful at marketing to Gazelles?

Harnish: Intuit is probably always the one that everybody sees as being the best.

Q: But hasn't their focus been more on the smaller end of the small business market?

Harnish: It has, but when they were able to go from Quicken to Quickbooks, they at least captured the sub-ten-million-dollar market in terms of Gazelles.

Q: What do they do right?

Harnish: First and foremost they have a great product. They know that small business owners talk with each other and that they have a very tight network. They also know that the first thing they do before making any decision is e-mail their buddies and say, "Hey, have you heard of this company? Have you had any experience with them? What do you think?"

Q: Why is their network so fundamental to reaching Gazelles?

Harnish: Because they don't have time to read. They don't have time to consider proposals, or look at their mail. They want firsthand experience. They want to know that there's somebody like them that is experiencing it. They have a sense that they're different than just your standard grocery store small business and at the same time know that they're not a large company. In fact, what makes them successful as a Gazelle is the fact that they are able to network their way into market customers and suppliers before making any kind of decision, especially the purchasing decision. So first and foremost Quicken has had the success in viral marketing, and clearly Seth Godin's ideas in his book *Ideavirus* and Gladwell's whole concept of "The tipping point," to me, applies more to the mid-market than the larger company or small business market. An example is Keith Alper, the past International President of YEO who founded the YEO chapter in St. Louis. He is what would be considered a connector and maven in Gladwell's terms. A connector knows everybody and a maven is seen as someone whose recommendations you can trust. Keith knows everybody and everybody knows Keith, and if Keith says it's good then a lot of people think it's good.

In addition, the CEOs of Gazelles tend to be the movers and shakers in their industries. For instance, Joe McKinney is the past President of his Wooden Pallet industry association. So, the way to reach gazelles is to get to the movers and shakers. They tend to be members of groups like Young Presidents' Organization (YPO), Young Entrepreneurs' Organization (YEO) and The Executive Committee (TEC). They're there because they want to grow their companies and they want to learn.

That's the way I know who runs a Gazelle firm and how I tell it in the MIT program I run. I can spot who is going to be a Gazelle and who are the Gazelles in that class pretty quickly, without even seeing the revenue numbers, by who seems to be taking it in, doing the notes, asking the questions, and who has read the material. They are the most voracious learners and that's why I say edu-commerce has such a huge future in reaching Gazelles. Because the Gazelles are hungry to learn and we're there to give them information that's going to help them make their business more successful. It's got to be from a business perspective, then you've got their attention and you've got a chance to sell them.

Q: What kind of learners are Gazelles?

Harnish: All different kinds. We use Harvard Professor Howard Gardner's seven intelligences to structure our learning approaches. When we're doing something with them we're trying to touch Gazelles on all seven intelligences. It's interesting, we've got a proposal with an organization to go out and see if we can establish how Gazelles think. They've got the standard tools to do that, but it's not a measure—they don't have a database on it. We don't know what they are thinking about.

Long-term, the key is putting the education in the flight path of people's work—this will be particularly important if you're going to use edu-commerce to reach the Gazelle market.

Q: So to go back to who has done a good job, Intuit started with a nice product and successful tapped into the network.

Harnish: They have a great product, and so therefore people talk about it and recommend it.

Q: What else did Intuit do right?

Harnish: The second reason pertains to a concept I got from John Cone at Dell University: they put their marketing in the flight path of your work. So the fact that it's in the software itself, it gives you more of an ability to connect, this will lead you to do more things.

Q: So if I'm understanding correctly, you go to pay your FedEx bill with Intuit and it says "Do you want to learn about FedEx shipping?"

Harnish: Yes, it's right in the flight path of doing the work, as opposed to mailing it out or sending you an e-mail.

Q: How do you communicate with Gazelles? Are there some hot buttons to push when crafting advertising for Gazelles?

Harnish: I think right now the best ad on the planet for reaching Gazelles comes from salesforce.com. The way to reach Gazelles is to feature Gazelles in your ads. You need to feature users of your product that Gazelles highly respect. So salesforce.com went out and put one of the founders of Hambrecht and Quist in their marketing material with a story of how Hambrecht and Quist chose salesforce.com.

If you want to reach Gazelles it's all about testimonials from people they respect. Nothing else matters to them. You can write up every feature and benefit you want and none of it matters. The reason why the "Birth of Giants" [Harnish's seminar for Gazelles] ad in *Inc. Magazine* works is because we list 50 companies who have graduated from the program. Gazelles are a bunch who rely heavily on referencing, so get your references up front. They like to see pictures of people they respect tied to your product or service, that's how you have to structure your ad and your mailers.

Gazelles act when they hear a recommendation from a reputable source. Nothing else. You could have the most beautiful brochure with the fanciest words and it doesn't matter. All they want to know is that someone they respect says it's okay.

Q: So what is it about the mindset of a Gazelle that make testimonials so important to them? What makes the Gazelle market any different from the "'Tween" market or the Baby

Boomer market? Why are testimonials not as important to those markets and so fundamental to this market?

Harnish: Because this market doesn't have time. I mean I'm amazed at how my mother will study things in order to make a decision. Even if it comes referenced from some movie star, she will still study it because she's got time. Our market has no time . . . they are moving so fast. These great entrepreneurs are rooted in reality. Those who make the best decisions are those that make decisions on real data. Michael Dell has grown his company because fundamentally he was closer and had more immediate data coming right from customers every week.

Q: So somehow marketers need to communicate real and believable success stories . . .

Harnish: That's what this bunch does: they're all about real experiences. Reality. It's even why the fundamental of a YEO forum group is that we must speak from experience. We don't want any theories or beliefs. You simply share your direct experience. That's why references are so important to Gazelles. If they speak to someone's direct experience with the product or service they will get their attention.

Q: And that's just because Gazelles don't have enough time?

Harnish: Yes, and because they want real data. I think the other thing is—we're such b.s. artists. We see through most marketing ploys because Gazelles are always marketing.

But there's the kinship among each other that says, "Hey, I don't want to recommend something to you that really isn't good because then I can't trust you to recommend to me something that's really good or not good." It's how we are. Gazelles assume they are being B.S.'d from a company that's trying to sell them. So if a Gazelle gets a third party off to the side who recommends something that turns out to be garbage, that Gazelle has just tarnished their own reputation. Gazelles understand that reputation is like virginity, you only lose it once. In the Gazelle market, we really do know that it's a small world. We know that we can't recommend something unless it's really good, or it just kills our own reputation and at the same time damages the network. So because of that, you can pretty much trust the recommendations of Gazelles.

Q. Are there any brands that really stand out as successfully capturing the imagination of the Gazelle market?

Harnish: I don't see any real brand loyalty. It tends to be very localized. By city because that's where Gazelles' networks tend to be. Ernst & Young has been very successful in Washington D.C. because of a guy named Bill Washecka. Every Washington-based Gazelle I know knows Bill Washecka. In fact it was big news in town that Bill Washecka retired from Ernst & Young. It rocked the city. It wasn't because of Ernst & Young; it was because of Bill Washecka at Ernst & Young. If you go to another town, Ernst & Young won't be as strong because the key man is from another firm. So it's very much the local personality that is associated with the brand that determines whether that firm makes it or not in the Gazelle market.

Q: So having said all of that, what advice would you give to Fortune 500 companies wanting to reach Gazelles?

Harnish: First off, have a great product that really gets Gazelles talking. Don't just "dumb down" your large enterprise product or try to "smarten up" your small business product, which is what Fortune 500 companies have a tendency to do.

Second, go out and find credible references from folks that are highly respected in the Gazelle market. Put them on all your marketing materials, including your ads. Actively reach the connectors and mavens that are out there. They are going to exist in a handful of organizations: Take YPO, YEO, The Executive Committee (TEC) and Council of Growing Companies (CGC) and you probably have access to almost all of the connectors and mavens you need. Those twenty thousand members are going to help you reach the other two hundred seventeen thousand Gazelles.

But it's very hard to get in with these groups. I've only seen a couple of people do it well, but one of the best displays came from a UPS representative named Glen at a recent National Association of Women Business Owners (NAWBO) conference. Glen works on the supplier diversity program for UPS and part of his job is to reach women business owners. It was clear that he had been at that conference for many years. They mentioned his name and the entire crowd gave Glen a standing ovation. And when Glen got up to speak to the women business owners, he shared with them information that mattered to them about their business. He wasn't up there pitching UPS as a delivery service. He was up there connecting with them saying, "Hey you've got a businesses to run, let me give you a couple of hints."

The reason I have credibility with the Gazelles I speak with is because I give them tools that are useful on Monday to help them run their businesses. Well, Glen from UPS has done the same thing with NAWBO, and as a result my sense is that UPS has a lot on those women businesses that FedEx doesn't; and those women talk a lot. The women that are members of NAWBO tend to be more aggressive and as a result UPS is going to extend its reach.

So, the problem is that Gazelles aren't formulaic enough and Fortune 500 companies need formulas. That's the only way they can think about reaching lots of folks. I feel that Seth Godin's new book, *Ideavirus,* and Gladwell's *The Tipping Point,* are truly the beginning to understanding how you can viral network your brand through the Gazelle market. (end of interview.)

Product Category	Mountain Climber Positioning
Gold and platinum credit cards	Think of it like an **all-access** pass to the game of business.
Blackberry, palm, or visor handheld organizers and wireless devices	Keep your fingers on the pulse of your business wherever you go.
Brand-name computers	Build your business on a solid foundation.
Traditional business banking services	Bank with someone who thinks "grow" is more than just a four letter word.
Sophisticated telecommunications services (e.g., high-speed Internet connectivity, data warehousing, e-commerce)	Nothing in your company moves slowly... so why should your data?

Figure 1.21 Selling to Mountain Climbers

Mountain Climbing Gear

Of the three psychographic profiles, most of our clients see Mountain Climbers as the most attractive segment of the small business market. They are growing and show potential to grow into larger, more profitable customers. Figure 1.21 shows an incomplete list of products that Mountain Climbers buy and the corresponding positioning likely to resonate with Mountain Climbers.

The trick to selling a product to a Mountain Climber is illustrating how it will help them grow.

Explain how it will help them grow.

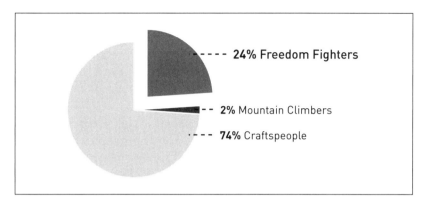

Figure 1.22 Breakdown of Small Businesses Owners by Psychographic Profile

Freedom Fighters

The second of the three psychographic profiles that make up the small business market is the Freedom Fighter (see Figure 1.22).

Freedom Fighters are motivated by independence. They do not want to build an empire—just a business that works. Freedom Fighters usually run companies that have between one and fifty employees. They tend not to change much from year to year, with flat annual revenue or modest growth of less than 20 percent per year.

Freedom Fighters go out of their way to avoid the side effects of growth that plague the Mountain Climber. For example, Mountain Climbers often find that they must answer to many people:

- nosy bankers who want to see receivables statements to make sure their money is safe
- angel investors who have given Mountain Climbers their money to help fuel their insatiable appetite for growth
- venture capitalists who often insist on having a say in

the way the company is run as a condition of putting
their skin in the game
- skilled partners and employees with whom they have
to share equity in order to retain them for the company's growth

To the Freedom Fighter, these shackles represent the
forces that they got into business for themselves to avoid.
Freedom Fighters simply can't stand having people tell them
what to do. Before starting on their own, Freedom Fighters
often spend years working for someone else, constantly
dreaming of ways they could run a better business if they
were in charge. This fierce sense of independence is why most
Freedom Fighters leave good jobs to work for themselves.
For Freedom Fighters, independence trumps growth.

All in the Family

Whereas Mountain Climbers are usually more autocratic in
their management style, Freedom Fighters are consensus
builders. They tend to hire friends and family or treat employees as if they were. Freedom Fighters often demonstrate
this paternalistic style by continuing to employ weak employees despite poor performance. This closeness is akin to
that in a family, making firing someone emotionally difficult.

I remember one interview with a Freedom Fighter named
Alan. Alan runs a small, five-person public relations firm and
is a classic Freedom Fighter. To understand Alan, you have to
go back a generation to get to know Alan's father who was a
very successful banker. Alan and his father enjoyed a close relationship until Alan was 14, when his father died suddenly.
Alan and his older sister were devastated. Alan's sister followed in her father's footsteps in the investment-banking
world. Alan took a different route. Although Alan enjoyed a
blue-blooded pedigree, a quick mind, and a wealth of connections—the usual prerequisites for a successful career on

Wall Street—Alan decided to forgo the money and prestige of banking to start his own company. Alan's independent streak was born out of a rebellion against the establishment that had taken his father's life so prematurely.

Today, Alan's company has five employees who are more like his family than his staff. They eat together, enjoy weekends at Alan's summer home, and all pitch in taking care of Alan's sheepdog (and office mascot), Whistler.

Once, Alan confided in me about an employee of his who was underperforming. He couldn't work out what to do. She seemed unmotivated and distracted and was often absent without explanation. If Alan were a Mountain Climber, he would have fired her months before, fearing that an underperforming employee would jeopardize his growth. But Alan is a Freedom Fighter and therefore continued to employ her for months longer than he should have.

To a Freedom Fighter, staff are like family.

David Leaves Goliath

I remember an interview with a Freedom Fighter named David. David used to work in England, where he was on his way to becoming an executive in a publishing company. He was a street-smart, thirty-something sales manager with an independent streak. David questioned most decisions his boss made and bristled under any degree of supervision or management.

One day, David decided he had had enough of working for a company that didn't seem to get it. He emigrated to North America, where he promptly started a distribution business from a spare bedroom in his house. David bootstrapped his company, moving from one industrial space to another. He never brought in any outside investors. He grew only as fast as his cash would take him.

After 18 years, David is now a successful Freedom Fighter with 20 employees. He works hard when necessary, but he also takes time to enjoy life. I had the opportunity to get to know David during a series of interviews in which his comments revealed a lot about the way Freedom Fighters think.

David was proud of the fact that he had succeeded on his own terms. He pointed out that the CEO of the company he had left earned less than David had last year, even though his former boss now managed ten times the number of employees. David seemed proud to have been responsible for his success. In fact, he left his salaried job because he wanted to succeed or fail on his own terms. He wanted to control the outcome rather than rely on the seemingly random decisions of most corporate hierarchies. He wanted to work in a meritocracy in which advancement was solely dependent on success, not on politics or dumb luck.

Today, you can see David's independent streak in everything he does, right down to his toes, which are exposed through a pair of sandals he wears to the office six months of the year. David pitches in with a variety of charities, including an AIDS hospice and a homeless shelter. He doesn't do it to impress anyone with his philanthropy; he has very little concern for what others think. David rarely wears a tie, swears like a sailor, indulges in a glass of good merlot at lunch, and drives a car with a supercharged motor—not exactly the habits of a corporate type saying the right things on the way to his next promotion. That is because David isn't trying to impress anyone. He's a Freedom Fighter, and the notion of doing things to impress people who oversee a system he doesn't control runs counter to everything he believes in.

Freedom Fighters march to their own drums.

Us versus Them

At its worst, Freedom Fighters' independent streak can manifest itself in a form of paranoia for anything they consider "establishment." They see the world through an intensely skeptical lens, referring to big business and government as "them" and looking suspiciously at almost any action "they" take.

I remember moderating one focus group full of Freedom Fighters. The group agreed that they did not see themselves as part of the business establishment, nor did they want to. They talked as though "they" (meaning big business and big government) were conspiring against them. This group harbored an intense skepticism about the motives of big business. All of the overtures made by big business wanting to serve small business were viewed by these Freedom Fighters as disingenuous attempts to win their pocketbooks.

Freedom Fighters are suspicious of your motives.

Top versus Bottom Line

When it comes to money, Freedom Fighters are more concerned with the bottom line than they are with the top. Whereas Mountain Climbers often spend freely today for the promise of tomorrow, Freedom Fighters live in the moment, preferring to maximize profitability today. As a result, they are more frugal than Mountain Climbers and make buying decisions slowly with more due diligence. You can find them at auctions, shopping around for a bargain on just about anything. This price sensitivity also means they are less likely to lease products in an effort to minimize financing expenses. Their sense of independence also makes them wary of being beholden to a financing company.

Mountain Climbers are defined by an intense inner need for personal achievement. Achievement in business means growth, and growth is usually defined in entrepreneurial circles by number of employees or top-line revenue. On the other hand, Freedom Fighters are less obsessed with achievement and therefore often don't feel the need to grow the top line at the expense of the bottom line.

Freedom Fighters see revenue as vanity and profit as sanity.

Status without Symbols

Although some celebrated examples of entrepreneurs are known for their flashy displays of wealth, most successful Freedom Fighters are modest about their money, using it as an internal gauge of their success as opposed to an external beacon. Dr. Thomas J. Stanley describes this phenomenon in his book *Selling to the Affluent*.[26] Stanley distinguishes between an affluent business owner and a wealthy professional such as a stockbroker or lawyer. Stanley suggests that the successful stockbroker or lawyer purchases prestige-oriented products as a badge of their superiority: a symbol of their respectability and a way of labeling themselves as successful operators within a profession that society often discounts as somewhat less respectable (heard any good lawyer jokes lately?).

This is in sharp contrast to the successful Freedom Fighter, who derives an enormous amount of self-confidence from the creation of a business. Combine what Maslow called "self-actualization" with the high levels of respect business owners are afforded in the community, and successful Freedom Fighters are much less likely to reach for status symbols to feel important. Dr. Stanley points to their desire to be recognized within their industry as a much stronger motivator than their desire to scream their success at the world at large.

Freedom Fighters don't fall for flash.

How Freedom Fighters Compete

Freedom Fighters believe their competitive advantage to be superior customer service and/or a unique product/service. If you talk to the owner of a local deli and ask him why his business hasn't been destroyed by the onset of McDonald's and Wendy's on every corner, he's likely to tell you one of two things: either his sandwiches are better or he knows his lunch crowd on a first-name basis.

---

26. Thomas J. Stanley. *Selling to the Affluent.* (New York: McGraw-Hill, 1991).

I can remember interviewing the owner of a four-person children's clothing retailer named Greg. He was a classic Freedom Fighter: fiercely independent, skeptical of big business, with a staff he referred to as his extended family. He lived in a city which offered lots of choices for buying kids' apparel—everything from the local department store to a variety of stand-alone children's clothing boutiques.

I asked Greg how he competes with all his larger, better-financed competition. Instead of answering the question directly, he opted to tell me a story about one Christmas Eve a few years before. The days leading up to Christmas were always hectic for Greg, with last-minute shoppers trying desperately to find that special something. As he was closing the store on Christmas Eve, Greg noticed a parcel sitting by the cash register. He opened it up and saw a sweater, which he remembered as the purchase of a good customer he knew well. Earlier that day, she had been in the store shopping for her grandchildren. In all of the pre-Christmas commotion, she had left her purchases in the store. Realizing the possible Christmas morning impact of this grandmother's forgetfulness, Greg hopped in his car after closing the store for the holidays and drove fifteen minutes to her home just outside of town so that she would have the gifts when her grandchildren came over for the big day.

A quaint story, to be sure, but also illustrative of what Freedom Fighters see as their competitive advantage. Greg remembered his customer's purchases well enough to match the abandoned bag with his long-time customer. He knew her address from their ongoing dealings and did not hesitate to drive out of his way on Christmas Eve to keep his customer for life.

Understanding how Freedom Fighters differentiate themselves from large competitors holds important lessons for marketers. Freedom Fighters are a tough audience. They offer unique products and services with fanatical customer service. In turn, they expect the same degree of attention from the suppliers they choose. Freedom Fighters tend to distrust and dislike banks, telephone companies, and computer makers largely because they cast their skeptical eye over these behemoths and hold them to the same standards of service they offer their own customers.

Freedom Fighters think their customer service is better than yours.

Staying under the Radar

The other explanation Freedom Fighters give for their success is that they offer a unique product or service: Luigi's pizza competes against that from the local Domino's because Luigi uses a special concoction of herbs and spices only he and his mother know how to make.

Many Freedom Fighters operate in tiny niches offering products and services so obscure, or in such local geographic markets, that they don't even register on the radar screen of their big business rivals. This highlights another important difference between Mountain Climbers and Freedom Fighters: Mountain Climbers have ambitions for growth and therefore pick products and services that give their companies the potential for growth in new geographic markets or for becoming substantial players in a particular industry. Freedom Fighters are content to stay on the sidelines, operating in relative obscurity, carving out an independent lifestyle with no visions of grandeur.

Freedom Fighters think local.

The Pursuit of Happiness

The differences between Mountain Climbers and Freedom Fighters go beyond their business lives. When it comes to leisure pursuits, Freedom Fighters exercise their need for independence, whereas Mountain Climbers seek out challenges.

You might find Mountain Climbers challenging themselves by running marathons and white water rafting. Look at the leisure choices of some celebrated Mountain Climbers: Richard Branson has a penchant for ballooning and has risked his life attempting to circumnavigate the globe in a hot air balloon. Larry Ellison, founder and CEO of Oracle, has competed (and won in 1995) in Australia's Sydney-to-Hobart race, a yachting race so intense that over the past three years, six sailors have died attempting to finish. Ellison is also an amateur pilot. Michael Clark, founder of Silicon Graphics, Netscape, and Healtheon pursues his interest for boats, but not just any boat—he challenged a team of Norwegian boat builders to build the largest yacht on the planet. After years of experiments, the vessel is now seaworthy and holds the world record for the yacht with the tallest mast. Peter Shea, the owner of *Entrepreneur Magazine,* not only chronicles the stories of entrepreneurs in the pages of his magazine, but also relaxes like one: Shea spends his weekends racing stock cars at 200 miles an hour.

The *Wall Street Journal* reports that Kay Koplovitz—the 55-year-old CEO of Working Women Network—enjoys a challenge too. After a hard week, Koplovitz relaxes by altitude hiking and white-water rafting in class-five waters.

These pursuits are not the normal fare of wealthy executives. Mountain Climbers seek the adrenaline rush of conquering a challenge in everything they do. Freedom Fighters, on the other hand, seek out independence in their leisure pursuits. They love individual sports like golf and tennis and enjoy traveling.

Know how your market has fun.

Freedom Fighting Weapons

Freedom Fighters can be an excellent target for many marketers. They are large enough (1 to 50 employees) to spend moderately on items that are important to them. They often run more stable companies than their Mountain Climber

Product Category	Freedom Fighter Positioning
Wealth management services (e.g., mutual funds, investment advice, etc.)	You've spent so many years taking care of everyone else—isn't it time you made sure you were taken care of too?
Group benefit plans	All good leaders give their teams peace of mind.
Credit cards with frequent flyer miles	Use the card for business and take the family away.

Figure 1.23 Selling to Freedom Fighters

cousins, keeping cash in the bank instead of constantly reinvesting in the business. Owners are often well-off personally, which opens up the entire wealth management category to marketers. Figure 1.23 shows an incomplete list of products that Freedom Fighters buy and the corresponding positioning likely to resonate with them:

The secret to selling to a Freedom Fighter is appealing to their need for independence, their paternal management style, and their sense of responsibility to their employees.

Freedom Fighters feel responsible.

Craftspeople

The third of the three psychographic profiles is a group we call Craftspeople (See Figure 1.24).

Craftspeople are so named because mastering their particular craft motivates them. They do not think of themselves as small business owners or entrepreneurs. Instead, they think of themselves in the context of their particular skill or service: as jewelers, plumbers, and photographers.

Craftspeople make up approximately 74 percent of the 21 million businesses in the United States. They typically work by themselves or with one or two part-time helpers.

The Craftsperson category of the small business market has experienced the largest growth over the past decade. This explosion has been caused by a combination of factors. First, technology has become so inexpensive that the individual can now afford to outfit a home office with computer equipment so powerful that only the largest of companies could have afforded it thirty years ago.

The second factor that contributed to the growth of the Craftsperson category was the recession of the early nineties. During a recession, large companies go about creating leaner, more tightly run organizations by downsizing (ironically, becoming more entrepreneurial in nature). As a result, new and smaller start-up companies begin to blossom—laid-off employees take their severance packages, along with their expertise, and start their own ventures.

Most of the businesses started by downsized employees are started by Craftspeople. According to a 1998 study done by the Small Business Administration, the largest increase in employment in the United States during the recession of 1990 to

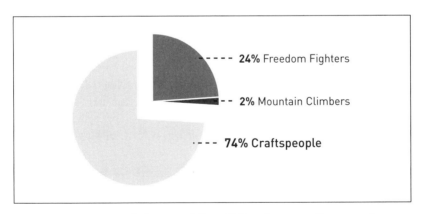

24% Freedom Fighters

2% Mountain Climbers

74% Craftspeople

Figure 1.24 Breakdown of Small Businesses Owners by Psychographic Profile

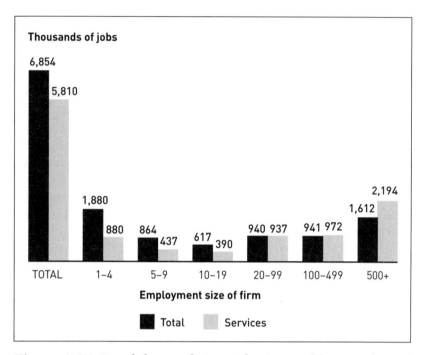

Figure 1.25 Breakdown of New Jobs Created by Number of Employees (1990–1995)
Source: Office of Advocacy of the U.S. Small Business Administration, *Statistics of U.S. Businesses,* provided by the U.S. Department of Commerce, U.S. Census Bureau.

1995 was in the one- to four-employee firm size class, where employment increased by 36.8 percent (see Figure 1.25).[27]

And in a Statistics Canada study, it was noted that, during the recession of the early 1990s, "nine-tenths of the newly self-employed were entrepreneurs working on their own without hiring any paid help."[28]

Whether you call them free agents, hired guns, free-

27. U.S. Small Business Administration, Office of Advocacy, *Statistics of U.S. Businesses,* provided by the U.S. Department of Commerce Bureau of the Census (Washington, D.C., 1998).

28. Lin, Zhangxi, Yates, Janice, Pico, Garnett, Statistics Canada Paper No. 133, *Rising Self Employment in the Midst of High Unemployment: An Empirical Analysis,* March 1999, 3.

lancers, SOHOs (small office/home office), consultants, or gurus, Craftspeople are reluctant entrepreneurs who would much prefer to practice their craft than think about managing a business.

I can remember moderating a focus group with eight Craftspeople. I started off with the requisite questions about what types of businesses they ran. Then I asked them to describe the hardest thing about being an entrepreneur. Two people in the group looked puzzled by my question. They squirmed a little bit and finally admitted they didn't really know how to answer. You see, they did not really think of themselves as entrepreneurs or business owners. They were Craftspeople and as such couldn't relate to my questions about being an entrepreneur.

The biggest chunk of the small business market is made up of individuals who do not even think of themselves as small business owners.

Price-Sensitive

Craftspeople are the most price-sensitive of the three psychographic profiles. The Craftsperson's stinginess stems from a simplistic approach to business.

Most Craftspeople do not distinguish their personal and business bank accounts in their mind. Many of them have separated their business banking on paper; in reality, however, they see their money as one big (or small) pot. As a result, purchases that would be considered a cost of doing business for Freedom Fighters and Mountain Climbers are postponed and considered for months by Craftspeople.

I remember interviewing one Craftsperson and the subject of her business card came up. She had been in business for three months and was researching the most cost-effective way to have business cards printed. She had investigated the local printer, Staples, and a friend who was a graphic designer. The research had taken her weeks, yet still she hesitated because she viewed the investment as a significant expense. She saw it as a few hundred dollars out of her pocket and every penny that she saved could be put towards other purchases, both personal and business.

As a marketer, you need to be realistic about your chances of selling to this sector. If you are a price leader in your category, go full steam ahead. If you are at parity with other players in your industry, proceed with caution. If, however, you're a premium-priced solution, think twice about selling to the Craftsperson market.

Craftspeople are bargain hunters.

The Guru on Gurus

To understand what Craftspeople are all about, take a look at this interview with guru.com's director of content Todd Lappin. Guru.com is a form of talent exchange through which Craftspeople register their services and receive connections to new projects. Lappin makes his living understanding what makes his members tick; he participated in this interview with marketingsherpa.com, an online marketing resource site:[29]

Q: How are independent professionals different from the rest of the small business marketplace?

Lappin: From a marketing standpoint, historically they've been lumped in with small business or SOHO. Those labels are completely inappropriate and counterproductive when you're figuring out how to talk to them. It's because there's a big difference between saying you want to be in the business of marketing your skills independently, and saying you want to be A Business. Those two don't have a thing to do with each other. In fact, gurus are small businesspeople

29. MarketingSherpa.com's MarketingToSmallbiz.com: *How to Market to Independent Professionals (Vs. Other Small Businesses), Practical Info on Marketing to the Millions of Small Businesses and SOHOs on the Internet* 11, no. 02 (14 January 2001).

who are in complete denial about being in business at all! They don't call themselves entrepreneurs. An entrepreneur is somebody who wants to build a business—who has some fantasy of having a little empire for themselves. Gurus are totally in it for lifestyle reasons. That is the thing you have to understand, or you'll miss the boat entirely.

Q: What works and what doesn't when it comes to appealing to this marketplace?

Lappin: Marketers are constantly trying to appeal to these gurus as small businesses, and this totally turns them off. They hate messages like, "Make extra income in your spare time" or "Here's how to grow your business" because the business part is the part they don't like. Gurus are very practical. They understand they are in business, obviously, but that's not really what turns them on. They have three core values you must appeal to:

- Freedom—the freedom to choose your own destiny, to allow your passion to be expressed in your work.
- Balance—striking a comfortable balance between work and life.
- Control—I don't want my fate to be tied to the fate of some corporation. I want to work on my own terms and be able to make as many of my own decisions as possible.

Q: How did you get so close to this marketplace?

Lappin: I've talked to hundreds over the past year. I write the Guru.com newsletter, so my personal e-mail address goes out to almost two hundred thousand people in every one. I get a lot of feedback! Plus we've done plenty of offline events all around the country in a bunch of major cities—L.A., Chicago, Boston, New York City, Seattle, Washington D.C.

Q: Wow, what did you learn from meeting these people in person?

Lappin: Gurus tend to be extremely unpretentious, laid-back people. A lot of "characters." They network naturally because they live or die by that, because historically they had to get by on word-of-mouth. I've never heard anybody say they do it for the money! They say, "I love my work, I'm more passionate, and guess what? I also make more money." That's as opposed to, "I want to make more money." That's what a small businessperson would say. Gurus strike a better balance between who they are and what they do for a living. It's a coincidence that you tend to make more money because you do better work. They are also really comfortable with uncertainty. They are risk takers. In that sense you can say they are entrepreneurial.

Q: How are the independent professionals you call gurus different from the SOHO marketplace?

Lappin: It's the same population ostensibly. It's become a marketing term associated with people who need staplers and personal printers. The term has blurred the line between a business and the spiritual aspirations of an independent professional. So it hasn't done anybody much good in terms of connecting with that audience.

Q: What marketing message works to reach independent professionals?

Lappin: Guru.com did a print magazine campaign that emphasized people working at home, but they were maybe sitting around the coffee table, or talking on the phone while standing on the back porch. The response we got was overwhelming! It wasn't "I completed my presentation because of this bubblejet printer." That's a reality, but not the part of their lives they really identify with. So if you want to reach them, you need to connect to the three core values. The printer will help you with the presentation and that sets you free. If you can take it one step further, it gets you somewhere. The presentation is a means to an end, not an end unto itself.

Q: What are the demographics of this audience?

78

Lappin: Men and women in their thirties and forties, but there's outliers. They tend to congregate in three broad areas:

- Tech, IT, and Web
- Creative industries like marketing
- Business consulting

So metaphorically it's the geeks, the black turtlenecks, and the button-down oxfords. However, there's a great degree of horizontal consistency. They might not dress the same but they are the same. There's an incredible amount of consistency of point of view and aspirations . . . what's success and what life's supposed to be about. Freelance marketers, java programmers, and business consultants are coming to realize that they have more in common with each other than they do with their counterparts in a corporate gig. So, you have an audience that's never been spoken to in the way they like to be spoken to before. When you connect with them, it's overwhelming! We do a thing called Guru Haiku. We encourage gurus to write haikus about their lives. It's staggeringly revealing about what these people are thinking about all day. It's told us an awful lot. I don't think it makes much difference where the people are from or what they do for a living. In those poems they say, "I love my freedom, and I'm a little worried about where the next paycheck is coming from." They write a lot about their pets. "The cat's sitting on the keyboard," or "the dog is my only officemate." They also talk about how much happier they are. So, there's incredible consistency regardless of geography or profession. The only difference is the geeks also do technology haiku.

Q: What sorts of companies should be targeting this marketplace specifically?

Lappin: Domain name registrars, health insurance, getting paid means collections services sometimes, personal technology, online access. You could also move pretty seamlessly into lifestyle-oriented stuff like clothing (although they lead Gap lifestyles and they're antifashion people in some ways). Travel services would do well—I imagine they do three-day weekend trips a lot. When you get a feel for the lifestyle aspect of their approach to work, you begin to understand what services these folks need most and how to connect with them. Just remember, it has absolutely nothing to do with entrepreneurship or small business! Small business is the last thing these people want to hear about.

Craftspeople are the un-entrepreneurs.

Craftspeople Tools

Many of our clients ignore this segment of the market, deeming it too small and unprofitable. That may be the case for some products, but for other categories, the craftsperson can be where the critical mass lies. Figure 1.26 shows an incomplete list of the types of products Craftspeople need.

Product Category	Craftspeople Positioning
Home computer	Inexpensive, reliable technology you don't need to think about.
High-speed Internet access	...Because your office is your castle.
Mobile phone	Make sure your clients can always be in touch.
Credit cards	Get discounts at our retail partners.

Figure 1.26 Selling to Craftspeople

Step #2: Find an Aggregator

After you have segmented the small business market into manageable chunks, you need to go out and find your slice of the pie.

Why is finding small business owners so difficult and acquiring them as customers so expensive? At the root of the problem lies a lack of consistency across the whole market. Because the small business market does not really exist, it is not surprising that no all-encompassing method can reach them. They do not all think alike, nor do they all watch the same television programs or visit the same web sites. To make things more difficult, small business owners are avid readers of trade magazines and local newspapers, so without advertising in hundreds of different publications, there is little hope of reaching all of your target market.

With no overarching way to reach small business owners, you need to supplement your traditional media buy with an aggregator that caters to your most profitable segments. We define an *aggregator* as a place where small business owners gather naturally without your having to drive them there. The trick to choosing an aggregator is to find somewhere that small business owners go naturally, because it defeats the purpose if you have to drive them to your aggregator. We've seen retail stores, office buildings, and parking lots being used as effective aggregators, but not all aggregators need to be in a physical location. We have also seen associations, web sites, and conferences act as effective aggregators.

Figure out where your slice of the small business market is aggregating.

How to Choose Your Aggregator

Aggregating to reach small business can provide you with more than just a larger prospect base. Savvy small business marketers choose an aggregator that can also help them address their marketing challenges. Specifically, aggregation can help overcome two key challenges:

1. If you have a complex product or service, a physical location as an aggregator can help you communicate a complicated offer through *high-touch* sales channels (i.e., live bodies to explain your offer in person).
2. If you compete in a highly competitive product category, an aggregator can often add a unique feature to your product to create a differentiated offer.

The type of aggregator you choose should depend on your particular marketing challenge. If your products or services are very complex or unfamiliar to the small business market, you should choose a partner that lets you get up close and personal with as many business owners as possible—a physical aggregator.

However, if your product or service falls into a very competitive, commodity-based category and you struggle for a point of differentiation, aggregate with those who can help you create new features that distinguish your offer from that of the competition.

Choose your aggregator based on your marketing challenges.

Reach Out and Touch Someone

Some products and services, generally those that are complex or unfamiliar to small business owners, are tough to sell using traditional marketing strategies, so you must find a physical aggregator.

I have seen companies try to pitch entrepreneurs everything from direct mail services to design services by phone or the web. Launching a direct mail program or designing a logo are relatively complex tasks involving many variables. Most owners would prefer to deal with someone personally. But marketers realize they cannot afford to offer one-on-one account management to small businesses, so they attempt to sell these complicated products through direct mail or the Internet. Such attempts fail because a more high-touch sales strategy is needed.

A physical aggregator can help you explain a complicated product or service without all of the traditional costs associated with one-on-one account management. Entrepreneurs gather naturally in some places—often the location of another small business service provider. Partnering with these companies gives you the chance to talk to your target personally.

ADP (Automatic Data Processing, Inc.), a payroll services company, found a great new high-touch sales channel for its complex service. In spring 2001, ADP and Staples announced a partnership that would enable ADP to set up information kiosks in all of Staples' 1,000+ retail locations in the United States. This partnership gives ADP a new face-to-face consultation channel reaching a large number of microbusinesses—the type of business most likely to do payroll in-house.

It also lets ADP reach both small business owners and their administrators, who are often responsible for payroll.

Although many small business owners would toss out an ADP mailer, they would be more likely to discuss their unique payroll questions with a live person. Mitch Gross, Staples' vice president of business services, claims that the increased foot traffic resulting from this partnership is greatly exceeding both companies' expectations.

When selling complex products or services, find an aggregator that allows for high-touch sales opportunities.

Get Them Where They Live

Another good way to aggregate small business owners physically is to get to entrepreneurs where they live. Savvy small business marketers are starting to create their own aggregation sites in the most unlikely of places: parking lots have become a great physical aggregator of small business owners. If strategically parked outside high traffic small business areas, a retrofitted 18-wheeler can be transformed into a mobile marketing center that can be used to go straight to entrepreneurs in their local community.

Remember that small business owners read local newspapers and think about their businesses in the context of where they live. This can be difficult for Fortune 500 marketers because they are used to thinking nationally (if not globally) with their marketing initiatives. In the small business market, you need to flip your thinking upside down and think bottom up.

The challenge of thinking locally is that it can be expensive and awkward to create and execute unique initiatives for hundreds of different towns and cities. Dell found a solution with its Dell on Wheels promotion, for which they outfitted an 18-wheeler complete with all of their latest servers and tech toys. Their traveling showroom tour visited 47 cities on the east and west coasts.

IBM Global Small Business launched the Small Business

e-Cities Tour, which featured a tractor trailer loaded with IBM goodies and staffed with smart Internet-savvy people. They toured cities across the United States, showing small business owners how they can use the Internet to improve their profits.

Wells Fargo turned an 18-wheeler into a rolling Internet banking kiosk, called the WellsFargo.com Bus. Once inside the kiosk, visitors are shown the power and simplicity of Internet banking and are asked to sign up for the Wells Fargo product.

Snap-on Tools—the stalwart supplier of every good independent auto mechanic shop—travels with most of its inventory in a specially designed truck that goes from shop to shop.

So think laterally when you're dreaming up your small business aggregator. It could be that parking a mobile marketing unit outside an area where small business owners are going is the best way to aggregate them locally.

Take your show on the road.

Combining Strengths

Let's recap: if your challenge is communicating a complicated offer to the small business market, look for a physical aggregator that will give you a high-touch sales channel. However, if your challenge is that you compete in a highly competitive, undifferentiated product category, you need to look for a partner that can add something unique to your offer in order to differentiate you from your rivals.

The company that sells specialized bolts to auto mechanics doesn't have to worry much about competition in the small business market. The uniqueness of the product guarantees that small businesses will keep coming back for the company's wares. If you are a telecommunications company hawking high-speed Internet access or a credit card company with a small business offer, however, the landscape looks very different. Competitors run rampant, and they continue to undercut your prices with special discount offers and improved customer service. In saturated markets, it is tough to find an attribute that will differentiate your product from everyone else's.

One way to distinguish yourself from the competition is to look for an aggregator with whom you can combine your strengths to create an offer unique in the marketplace. The partnership between Pfizer, IBM, and Microsoft (outlined next) is a great example of three powerhouses coming together to create a product that none of them could produce individually.

Use your partner's strengths to create an offer that is unique in the marketplace.

Defining Your Market Space

Early in 2001, IBM and Microsoft chose pharmaceutical giant Pfizer as a small business aggregator, which not only gave them cost-effective access to the small business market but also helped them develop a unique, highly differentiated offer.

Pfizer, Microsoft, and IBM joined forces to create a new company to sell Application Service Provider–based (ASP-based) software to physicians in small practices, many of whom cite "improving operating efficiencies" as a primary concern.[1] The software is designed to address their concerns through automated physician record keeping, including functions to manage their appointment schedules, patient medical histories, referrals, and prescriptions.

The partnership offers great opportunities to all of the companies involved. Pfizer gets to expand its product offering by leveraging its knowledge of the medical market. Microsoft and IBM, both of which have health-care divisions that target the larger end of the physician community, will gain a powerful new distribution channel among small practices.

1. Health Management Systems Society, *11th Annual HIMSS Leadership Survey,* Sponsored by IBM Final Results web site, 2000.

Joining forces to create an innovative product or service allows you to bring something new to the market that one company could not create on its own. Pfizer would be hard pressed to create software without Microsoft, and IBM and Microsoft benefit from Pfizer's access to small medical practices. Together, however, the three companies are able to create a product that could potentially revolutionize the small physician market.

Partnership can give you a whole new market.

Making Friends in the Right Places

Another way to aggregate the small business market is to build contacts with business owners' favorite associations. Generally speaking, associations can be one of two types: (1) a vertical association that is dedicated to serving a specific industry (e.g., The American Bar Association serves lawyers) and (2) a horizontal association organized to serve all business owners in a certain location (e.g., Greater Miami Chamber of Commerce). Vertical associations have the benefits of being able to target a specific message to a specific industry. Horizontal associations are best used when your offering is appropriate for a specific geographical area or will appeal to all business owners.

Our company did a ranking of the top 50 associations in the United States that make fitting partners for small business marketers. We used a variety of criteria to rank the top associations. Our five most attractive associations from a marketing standpoint were:

- National Federation of Independent Business— 600,000 members
- American Bar Association—400,000 members
- American Farm Bureau Federation—5,000,000 members
- American Dental Association—144,000 members
- National Small Business United—65,000 members

When you size up an association to seek as a partner, consider the following indicators of a healthy potential partner:

- Number of members: for most Fortune 500 marketers, the more members the better.
- Percentage of membership that own a business: many associations accept anyone from their industry or area regardless of whether they are the owner of the business. This usually results in a lot of members, many of whom are not owners, and therefore diminishes the efficiency of the partnership for you. Look for a high percentage of owners.
- Average size of a member's business: generally, the larger the average business is, the more attractive a partner.
- Membership growth rate: the pace at which the association is growing helps to indicate its overall health.
- Average annual renewal rate: generally speaking, the higher the renewal rate the better. However, if members have to join the industry association in order to practice a profession, ignore this statistic; in those situations the number is generally very high and does not indicate the health of the organization because members are forced to renew to keep practicing.
- Membership fees: generally speaking, the higher the fees, the more engaged an audience. Again, be careful with professional associations that businesspeople must join to practice their professions (e.g., American College of Physicians).
- Access: the more points you have available to access the membership, the better. When you strike a deal, insist on coverage in newsletters and web sites and exposure at events, and ask about the availability of direct snail mail and e-mail lists.

Association marketing is not as pretty as mass advertising and it doesn't exactly make for scintillating conversation, but given the importance of finding efficient ways of reaching

small business owners through aggregation, association marketing should be part of your small business attack plan.
Size up your partners.

Three Wins

Some Fortune 500 companies have created entire armies of senior staffers whose sole responsibility is to cut deals on behalf of the company with groups representing large numbers of small business owners. The secret to a worthwhile deal is convincing the association to mention the partnership at every turn.

IBM is one of the pioneers in the area of association marketing, and I spoke with the executive who led the association team in the spring of 2000. Steve Wittenborn told me what he looks for in a deal: "My definition of a successful partnership is one that provides me with excellent access to the association's membership," Wittenborn says. "I'm looking for someone who is committed to getting our message through on an ongoing basis, whether it's through e-mail, the association newsletter, advertisements, or conferences."

Wittenborn went on to say that partnering with an association should be a three-win situation: "The association membership is looking for good deals and good information. The alliance has to get something out of it as well, in terms of both nondues revenue and customer/membership satisfaction. And we want the association to make sure their members are aware of what we're trying to market. It's a win for us, a win for the association, and a win for the small business members."

Steve Wittenborn has also had his share of bad experiences with partnerships and explains why they fail: "They [associations] didn't communicate our message often enough and didn't have a real interest in our success. There just wasn't enough focus on adding this kind of value to their membership."

Ralph Lynn, Director of Alliance Marketing for NEBS

Canada, also stresses a long-term relationship: "The fact is, seventy percent of alliances fail after three years," reflects Lynn. "For one thing, people go in expecting immediate results. They don't realize that building a relationship and getting results take time. When one side doesn't see those results right away, distrust sets in—and that's when you're doomed to failure."

Lynn's advice to Fortune 500 marketers seeking to expand their reach in the small business market through association marketing is to do thorough research into the association. Talk to its members—get feedback on the benefits of membership and where the members see room for improvement. And as part of your research, look for those associations that don't force small business owners to join in order to practice their profession. If small business owners are members of an association only because they are required to do so, you may have a less enthusiastic audience for your marketing message.

Wondering what the associations look for in return for providing access to their members? Bernie Butler is the vice president of marketing, development, and technology for the National Federation of Independent Business (NFIB) and holds the key to one of the largest small business groups in the United States. In the spring of 2000, I asked Bernie what he looks for in a deal on behalf of his 600,000 members: "When it comes right down to it, our members have two concerns. They want to meet payroll on Friday, and they want efficient ways to get their work done," says Butler. "So when we look for partnerships, we look for someone who can provide the kind of resources that will help members do exactly those things."

Give someone the job to make friends.

Co-Branding for Credibility

Fortune 500 companies often ask us how best to communicate to the members of a small business association. As such, they wonder whether a marketing message should come from the association, the marketer, or both.

To find out, we ranked the top 50 associations in North

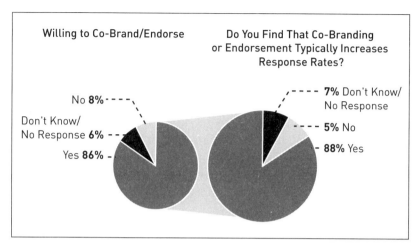

Figure 2.1 Relationship between Association Co-Branding and Response Rate

Source: Warrillow & Co., *"The Leverage Effect:* A Ranking of the Top Associations and Chambers of Commerce for Reaching Small Business Owners." *Warrillow Report,* Vol. 10, Issue 03, Toronto, 2000.

America[2] and asked them to offer advice to Fortune 500 companies interested in marketing to their members. One of the most resounding suggestions was to co-brand all offers with the branding of both the association and the marketer on any communication.

Association executives reasoned that, by co-branding, the marketer leverages the goodwill between the association and its members. In fact, 86 percent of the associations we asked in preparing the study allowed marketers to co-brand their offers. Of those who allowed the practice, 88 percent said response rates typically improved when marketers co-branded their communication (see Figure 2.1).

Never underestimate the power of trust in the small business market.

Leverage trust wherever possible.

2. Warrillow & Co., "The Leverage Effect: A Ranking of the Top Associations and Chambers of Commerce for Reaching Small Business Owners," *Warrillow Report* 01, no. 03.

The Hierarchy of Networking

So you've decided to make association marketing one of your tactics this year—good. Now you must understand the hierarchy of networking in the small business market.

The hierarchy principle illustrates that not all associations are created equal. For marketers, the more exclusive and successful an association's membership, the more attractive. The most exclusive associations have erected barriers of entry which are designed to keep wanna-bes out (see Figure 2.2 for an illustration of the exclusivity hierarchy of business associations).

The most common and easiest associations for small business owners to join are Chambers of Commerce. Entrepreneurs looking to network or get discounts on certain products or services join their local Chamber of Commerce. The next level up are nonprofessional trade/industry associations that small business owners join to network with their peers and get news and education related to their industry. To join

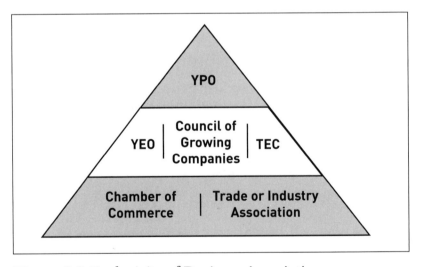

Figure 2.2 Exclusivity of Business Associations

these associations, a business needs to be in the specific industry connected with the association.

The farther you go up the pyramid, the more attractive, yet more exclusive and secretive these clubs get.

Mountain Climbers are more likely to join one of a hierarchy of peer-to-peer networks. Before gaining acceptance into the Young Entrepreneurs' Organization (YEO), a business owner needs to be under 39 years old and be the founder, cofounder, owner, or controlling shareholder of a business with sales of a million dollars or more. Or, if you're a recent start-up, to join YEO you must have raised two million dollars in private capital or five million dollars in publicly raised funds, have at least 10 employees, and reach at least one million dollars in gross annual sales within three years of joining. Young Presidents' Organization (YPO) members must be under 50 (and under 44 when applying for membership) and have at least 50 full-time employees, or a total employee compensation package of one million dollars or greater. Sales criteria vary greatly by industry but start at around six million dollars.

Groups like The Executive Committee (TEC) and the Council for Growing Companies cater to similarly exclusive groups.

Many small business marketers build off-the-shelf discount programs for all associations in an effort to minimize the cost of structuring hundreds of different deals; that strategy works fine for generic associations. But the higher you go up on the hierarchy of networking, the less likely these cookie-cutter deals are to be successful. The exclusive groups know their members are in demand and will not settle for the same discount package you offered the members of the Dayton Chamber of Commerce. Consorting with the more exclusive groups requires a willingness to build a special and exclusive deal just for their members.

The higher you go, the tougher the climb and the better the view.

Why Small Business Trade Shows Are a Bad Aggregator

Don't waste your money sponsoring small business trade shows unless your audience is pre–start-up, wanna-be entrepreneurs. Legitimate entrepreneurs don't go within a mile of these shows. Even though the marketing of such shows talks about "growth strategies" and "managing staff," the only people who actually go are nine-to-fivers looking for an escape hatch.

Does this mean entrepreneurs don't like to network? No, quite the opposite. In the United States, The National Foundation of Independent Business boasts over 600,000 members. Almost every city large enough to appear on a map has a chamber of commerce to help local business owners network. In fact, we worked with one bank whose most successful event of all time was a business card exchange in which they invited entrepreneurs from all over town to attend for the express purpose of exchanging business cards with other business owners. The result was a networking Olympics, an unapologetic schmooze fest for successful business banking clients.

Yes, entrepreneurs love to network, but they look for networking events where they can find people at (or just beyond) their level in terms of the size and scope of their business achievements. They want give-and-take networking relationships. The problem with trade shows is that just anyone can go, and everyone does except for legitimate business owners. With no barriers to entry, small business trade shows quickly deteriorate into a collection of dreamers touring an endless row of so-called franchise opportunities and network marketing schemes.

Real business owners steer clear of small business trade shows because they want to network with people who are in a similar business situation. Tennis provides a good analogy: play with someone who is just learning and it is the most frustrating sport on earth; take on a player like Pete Sampras and you'll be embarrassed. The trick is to find an opponent who will stretch you a bit, but not too much.

The same holds true for entrepreneurs. They choose events that offer the opportunity to meet other business owners who are at approximately the same level as they are.

A great example is the success of Ernst and Young's Entrepreneur of The Year Award Program, responsible for the highest-profile event in entrepreneurship. At the annual awards ceremony held in California every year, the action takes place in the breakout sessions that accompany the awards dinner. In these breakout sessions, nominees and past winners get together in small groups to learn from each other. The energy is contagious.

Ontario's Ministry of Economic Development, Trade, and Tourism's most successful event in its history is the annual "Wisdom Exchange." Instead of hearing from high-profile ministers or corporate leaders, entrepreneurs participate in the action by forming forum groups to learn from one another's experiences.

Small business events can make great aggregators, but look for sponsorship events for which the organizers have erected a barrier to entry for potential small business applicants. Such a barrier could be a minimum number of years in business, specified sales volume, accredited industry membership, or minimum number of employees—and the environment will give your brand a halo effect. Sponsor another generic small business trade show and you end up reaching just a hopeful group of tire kickers.

Only sponsor events that have a barrier to entry.

Nuts and Bolts

Many of our clients experiment with event marketing as a way to aggregate the small business market. Done right, event marketing can be a great way to generate good buzz, position your brand in the vanguard, and collect a database of entrepreneurs for follow-up initiatives. But why do some events succeed while most fail to draw any real following?

The first secret is to erect a barrier to entry for attendees to minimize the presence of those who are not real business owners. The second trick to organizing a successful event in the small business market is to impart business owners with practical information and tools they can immediately use in their businesses.

I was fortunate enough to attend a program called "Birthing of Giants" offered by a partnership between MIT, YEO, and *Inc. Magazine.* Every year, 62 entrepreneurs from around the world are invited to attend this event that offers an intense four-day program. Watching the entrepreneurs in the room absorb the sessions revealed much about what business owners want from an event.

The speakers on the docket generally broke out into three categories:

- academics
- successful entrepreneurs
- subject-matter experts in the area of motivating employees, growth strategies, and team building

While the academics spoke, most of the entrepreneurs in the room listened politely and a few found excuses to get up and check their voice mail. The successful entrepreneurs who spoke were interesting and the audience was more engaged.

The entire mood changed, however, when the subject-matter experts started to speak. Formerly restless entrepreneurs started to take notes and became fully attentive. Attendees were hunched over their desks scribbling every word offered and lapping up every insight dispatched. Most subject-matter experts were forced to stop fielding questions from eager participants in order to complete their presentations.

What happened here? Why would a successful entrepreneur not be more interesting than a subject-matter expert? The difference can be distilled down to three words: *nuts and bolts.* The subject matter experts were offering attendees real, practical advice they could put to work in their businesses that day. The businesspeople in the room were too concerned

96

about making their businesses succeed today to listen to philosophical musings or hear another Pollyanna story from a successful entrepreneur.

Nuts and bolts are why *Inc. Magazine* outsells its closest rival in the small business magazine business for advertising pages almost two to one in most years. Entrepreneurs want to know how. They react to fires daily and rarely get the luxury of looking beyond next quarter; as a result, they enjoy content that tells them how to do so.

About the worst event-marketing mistake you can make is to invite politicians, corporate managers, or bureaucrats to speak to entrepreneurs. Banks are notorious for this blunder. They host lunches, invite speakers, and generally try to suck up to the small business community. They invest millions into motherhood-and-apple pie marketing. These events come complete with warm and fuzzy speeches from politicians, lobby groups, and all manner of hangers-on. They're incestuous outings with the same people (the only real-life entrepreneurs in attendance are bank suppliers) showing up every time.

I saw the entrepreneur's characteristic disdain for anything but practical advice play out at a meeting of the International Small Business Congress. This worldwide gathering of entrepreneurs had grown from an underground meeting of 125 delegates in 1974 to a festival of entrepreneurship with over 1,000 disciples journeying from 50 countries to Toronto in the year 2000.

I attended as a fly on the wall. Along with a healthy contingent of small business owners, the four-day event attracted many academics, government folks, and corporate types. As soon as the coffee breaks came, the entrepreneurs in the room swarmed to one another, furiously trying to exchange thoughts, ideas, and leads, leaving the bankers and bureaucrats idly chatting among themselves on the perimeter.

If you plan to organize events as a way to aggregate the market and ingratiate your company with the small business community, keep your executives off the stage. Leave the politicians cutting ribbons at the mall and bolster your company's reputation by inviting speakers who have real tools to share with entrepreneurs.

Business owners are thirsty for nuts-and-bolts advice they can use today.

The Buzz on Buzz

One essential component to any aggregation strategy is the word-of-mouth talk that percolates whenever entrepreneurs get together in person. At its best, this word-of-mouth marketing, or *buzz,* can be the lubricant that spreads the word about a good product faster than any advertising campaign; at its worst, bad buzz among entrepreneurs can be the acid that corrodes any chance of a marketing program's success.

Whether they are at an association meeting, at a small business event, or in line at Staples, business owners talk. They value the opinions of their peers. They exchange stories about their businesses, compare experiences with certain products or suppliers, and offer each other tips on the best deals on everything from PCs to paper towels.

In fact, The Young Entrepreneurs' Organization (YEO)— arguably the most successful not-for-profit association serving entrepreneurs—is built around the concept of peer groups known simply as *forums.* Each forum group is made up of 8 to 10 entrepreneurs that meet each month to discuss whatever is on their minds. The group is sworn to a strict code of secrecy—loose-lipped members are removed immediately. Even discussion in a forum group is governed by a series of rules whereby entrepreneurs must take ownership of their comments instead of giving advice. For example, a forum group member must not start a sentence with "you should do—." Instead, they must speak from their own experience by saying "in my experience, I have found that—."

Entrepreneurs discuss just about anything with their forum groups: partnership disputes, marital problems, bankruptcy, going public, substance abuse. Just about every possible challenge an entrepreneur could face, professionally or personally, has been addressed in a forum group at some point in time.

In the same way entrepreneurs rely on each other for business advice and peer counsel, they also lean on the same network when choosing suppliers. This buzz is one of the most powerful tools in influencing the buying decisions of small business owners.

Emanuel Rosen, author of *The Anatomy of Buzz: How to Create Word of Mouth Marketing,* defines buzz as "all the word of mouth about a brand. It's the aggregate of all person-to-person communication about a particular product, service or company at any point in time."[3]

In order to generate a good buzz about your company, you need to influence the buzzkeepers of the small business market. *Buzzkeepers* are those people who influence the buying decisions of small business owners.

Your sales channel can be one of the most important buzz-keepers to influence. According to Christopher Plonka, who studies small business network solutions at Bowie State University, 72 percent of small business owners who use a Value-Added Reseller (VAR) follow the recommendations they receive (see Figure 2.3).[4]

Other buzzkeepers include editors of small business publications like *Inc.* and *Fortune Small Business,* industry association executives, business leaders, and educators at entrepreneurship schools like Babson College's Arthur M. Blank Center for Entrepreneurship and MIT's Entrepreneurship Center.

Of course, entrepreneurs themselves generate the best buzz of all. It's also the most difficult buzz to influence. We work with one technology company that has formed a small business advisory council made up of leading entrepreneurs

3. Emanuel Rosen, *The Anatomy of Buzz: How to Create Word of Mouth Marketing.* (New York: Doubleday, 2000), 7.

4. Christopher Plonka, Bowie State University, Small Business Networking: A Market That Is No Longer Being Ignored. Retrieved August 2001. Available from http://faculty.ed.umuc.edu/~meinkej/inss690/plonka.htm.

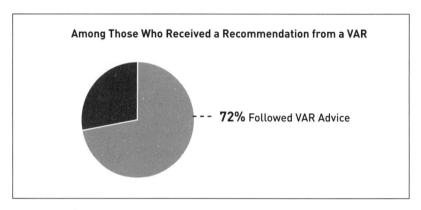

Figure 2.3 Percentage of VAR Customers Who Follow VAR Advice

Source: Plonka, Christopher, Bowie State University, *Small Business Networking: A market that is no longer being ignored*, VAR Business, 1998.

with high profiles in their communities. The council is large and diverse, having members in most major United States cities. They selected what they call thought leaders who are successful and progressive—the kind of big-idea people who often influence trends and others' thoughts.

This company outfits each council member with new products, has them beta test new ideas, and generally treats its council as ambassadors. No major marketing decision is made without the feedback of the council. The result has been an authentic underground buzz started by council members who have become evangelists for this technology company. The council has also allowed this technology company to generate interest in new products without alerting its competition too early with a noisy advertising campaign.

The key to the company's success in this undertaking was the authenticity of the council's role. Too many marketers latch on to the idea of a small business advisory panel and use it for little more than a public relations ploy. This underestimates the value of having a group of evangelists spreading good buzz about your company. In the case of the aforementioned technology company, its advisory council worked because the members played a legitimate consulting role. The ad people listened when the group thought a campaign was off-strategy, and the product designers actually changed their plans when beta versions flopped with the council. If you are planning a small business advisory panel as a publicity stunt, you underestimate the other buzz benefits available when you mobilize a group of entrepreneurs in favor of your brand.

An aggregation strategy lives or dies by the buzz that defines it. Many buzzkeepers can affect your strategy's success, but the most influential—and toughest to convince—are the small business owners themselves.

Other entrepreneurs can be your most powerful sales tool or most destructive deal breaker.

Reactive Buyers

The importance of finding an aggregator that allows you constantly and physically to be in the face of the small business market is underscored by the fact that business owners are reactive buyers. Unlike big businesses that operate from procurement schedules, forecasts, and well-laid plans, entrepreneurs buy your products and services when they feel the need.

Consider, for example, computer equipment. In most large companies, the purchasing department proactively prepares a schedule of when systems will need to be updated. A few months prior to the targeted purchase date, the company sends proposals to a handful of trusted suppliers. People in the purchasing department then review the bids, comparing matters like price and service, then prepare a recommendation for their boss—very orderly.

In a small business, the decision to purchase computer equipment is often reactive rather than proactive; for example, a new hire is starting Monday or an old system crashes, making a key staffer unproductive. Because an urgency usually surrounds the purchase, the decision is made quickly with less due diligence.

The process works the same way in other sectors. Small business owners feel the need for credit when they max out their lines. They need courier services when a package must arrive tomorrow. They want three-way calling when they have just scheduled a conference call.

Be in their face when they feel the need.

The Local Rag

When it is time to plan your media buy to supplement and promote your aggregation initiatives, remember that small business owners think locally. They want to keep in touch with the news in their own communities, so they generally consume more locally focused media like radio and local newspapers. They catch up on local news and politics before they consider vacillations at the Federal Reserve or musings of Washington. In fact, our company studied the media habits of small business owners and learned that 81 percent of small business owners claim to read a large metro newspaper at least three times per week, whereas only 26 percent claimed to read a national paper regularly.

The same trend applies to magazines. A national business magazine like *Fortune* claims only one in four of their readers are small business owners. However, regional business magazines like *Southern California Business Life* (most regions have their own) claim that more than 95 percent of their readers are small business owners.

The one exception to this rule is Mountain Climbers, who see themselves growing onto a national stage and are therefore more likely than other entrepreneurs to read a national newspaper. In fact, to meet this demand from Mountain Climbers, national business bible the *Wall Street Journal* launched a series of articles in April 2001 called "The Challengers" to cater to this elite group of business owners.

Most small business owners think local.

Double Your Pleasure

Most Fortune 500 marketers targeting the small business market do not localize their messaging, even though today's direct-marketing technology makes it simple and relatively inexpensive. I can remember consulting with a major United States bank who had requested our help because it had been getting consistently lower and lower response rates on its direct-mail promotions. We examined the bank's product offering, which proved solid, and we established that it was working from a reputable list. Therefore, we focused our attention on how this bank was talking to prospects. The bank's direct-marketing copy was very generic, referring to "small business owners" and their "financial needs."

We suggested the bank make one change; the company was to localize the copy to include the name of the city where the business owner lived on the outside of the envelope. For example, a business owner who lived in Denver would receive an envelope reading *special offer for Denver business owners.*

That one change doubled the response rate.

Small business owners think locally, and the more you can prove to them that you are part of their local business communities and that you understand their cities, the more success you will have.

Talk local.

CHAPTER 3

Step #3: Speak Their Language

Now that you have segmented the market and found a way to aggregate small business owners, you need to start communicating with them.

Talking to entrepreneurs is made more difficult because of the fragmentation of the small business market. No one formula guarantees effective communication with business owners. However, after moderating hundreds of small business focus groups and conducting thousands of interviews with entrepreneurs, we have discovered some general commonsense guidelines that seem to extend across the entire small business market.

Some communications basics apply across the board.

Small Business Owner?

Calling someone a "small business owner" in your marketing communications is a big mistake.

Consider this: the American Institute of Certified Public Accountants (AICPA) did a poll asking small business owners what they would do with a sudden profit of one million dollars.

Forty-four percent replied "pay down debt." Twenty-two percent said "expand facilities," and another 13.2 percent said "expand staff." Only 20.3 percent said they would increase their own salaries/bonuses.[1]

Ask some average consumers what they would do with a million dollars and they'll tell you about the exotic places they would visit, the European cars they would buy, and the homes they would build. Yet over 80 percent of small business owners would put that money right back into their companies. People who would forgo almost everything to see their businesses succeed do not take kindly to being referred to as a "small" anything.

It's not a *small* business if you own it.

One game I like to play when I talk to small business owners is to ask them what they do for a living. The most common answer I hear is something that refers to their expertise: "I'm an architect" or "I'm in the computer business". Occasionally I hear a reply like "I own a manufacturing business" or "I have a company that sells wholesale T-shirts." I have done thousands of interviews with small business owners, and I can count on one hand the number of people that have identified themselves as "small business owners."

So if you can't call them small business owners, what should you call them? Try simply *business owner, CEO, entrepreneur, founder, president*—anything but *small business owner.* If you know which type of small business owner you are trying to reach, so much the better:

- Craftspeople™: Refer to them by profession—*massage therapist, architect,* or *plumber.* Craftspeople are

---

1. American Institute of Certified Public Accountants (AICPA), Private Companies Practice Section, *Sixth Annual Survey of Small Business Decision Makers,* 1996.

more proud of their skills than they are of owning a business.

- Freedom Fighters™: They have businesses with payrolls, leases, and lines of credit. Their businesses are small by almost any standard except their own. To Freedom Fighters, nothing is small about their businesses; you should refer to them simply as *business owners.*

- Mountain Climbers™: They are attempting to grow an important business. Therefore, they are even less likely to think of themselves as small in any respect. Instead of *small business owner* use *entrepreneur, founder, CEO,* or *president.*

Don't be afraid to refer to small business in the third person, as in "this widget is perfect for a small business that makes X." They have the self-awareness to know their own business is smaller than most, but they will think more highly of a company that acknowledges the difference between a small company and a small person.

Never call them small business owners.

Missing Them All

One of the worst communications images used in small business marketing is that of a young boy wearing a men's suit. By using this image, marketers intend to imply that their product or service can help a new company become a big (grown-up, so to speak) company one day. I have seen this image of a boy wearing an oversized men's suit used with slight variations to sell everything from Internet access to banking services. This one image is completely inappropriate because it manages to alienate all three kinds of business owners:

- Craftspeople make up approximately three-quarters of the small business market. They are motivated to be the best at what they do and have no interest in growing a big business. Talking to them about a baby business that might one day mature into a full grown business misses the point.

- Freedom Fighters are motivated by independence. They don't want to grow bigger for bigger's sake. They are striving for a business that will give them freedom, both professional and personal. Most of them left the corporate world to avoid the structure of being managed. The men's suit used in these ads is one of the oldest icons of corporate America—the very place they have tried to escape.

- Finally, Mountain Climbers take offense at this imagery and its implication that their business is childish, insignificant, and immature. Mountain Climbers are ego-driven builders and obsessed with challenging themselves. They are looking to grow a business and they tie an enormous part of their self-worth to its success. To talk down to a Mountain Climber as a goofy child hoping to grow is a mistake.

So before you run the ad with the boy in the oversized suit or the kids at the lemonade stand, remember that this imagery is seen as irrelevant at best and offensive at worst.

Shelve the suits and lemonade stands.

Walking the Line

Addressing the small business market can be a delicate balancing act—marketers must walk a thin line between getting too technical and being too condescending. And according to Rick Spence, who makes his living communicating with entrepreneurs as the Editor and Publisher of *PROFIT* magazine, it's not a task marketers perform well: "A common mistake among Fortune 500s is that they either talk down or talk up to the small business audience."

Spence believes that, despite warnings to the contrary, many marketers are still belittling this audience with the term *small*. "Many business owners think, 'a small business is any business smaller than mine,'" he says. It was this principle that led the magazine to change its name to *PROFIT* from *The Magazine for Small Business* 10 years ago.

"'Small business' is a marketing category, a label," Spence goes on to explain. "The government might classify someone as a 'repeat offender,' but you probably wouldn't want to address them that way."

On the other hand, Spence believes that many marketers also overestimate the level of technological savvy among entrepreneurs. Although most business owners are well-educated professionals, the bulk of their knowledge lies squarely in a specific trade or product. Communications aimed at the small business market should be written in simple language without industry jargon or technical terms.

"Small business owners won't necessarily know what an 'enterprise-class CRM [customer relationship management] solution' is, or what it can do for their business," says Spence. Be sure to spell out the benefit. The key is to use simple language without being simplistic or condescending.

They know their business, not yours.

Cliché

"Let's have some new clichés."
—Samuel Goldwyn

Over the past few years, marketers have done their homework. Through thousands of focus groups and hundreds of surveys, they have concluded that small business owners are busy multitaskers that collectively make up an important part of the economy.

So in an effort to show they empathize with these entrepreneurs' plight, marketers have attempted to demonstrate their unique understanding in their marketing communications messages. Unfortunately, what were all solid insights a few years ago have now become forgettable clichés:

- *You're busy, so we'll get right to the point.*
  This is a favorite introductory line used by telephone and credit card companies in their direct mail letters.
- *You wear many hats: you're the CFO, the CEO, the Vice President of Marketing and the janitor.*
  Somewhat funny and relevant a few years ago, today this line is tired. Within a short time, Hertz, Register.com and Kinko's have all used the same idea with a slightly different execution.
- *Small business owners like you are the engine of our economy.*
  This little gem pops up in almost every financial services brochure ever written. Ignore it—your target does.

The small business owner is so used to seeing clichés like these, such lines have become marketing wallpaper; small business owners don't even notice them anymore.

The war for the small business market has hit the mainstream. Every major technology company, telecommunications giant, financial services institution, and office product purveyor wants a piece. The winners will be those who depart from these tired old lines and uncover the next generation of fresh insights.

Keep it fresh.

Driving the Economy?

Talking about the economic contribution of the small business sector is great fodder for politicians, economists, and academics, but it does not win you any points with entrepreneurs.

Pick up almost any marketing piece targeted to the small business owner and you are sure to find a gushing (if not patronizing) reference to their importance to the economy. The underlying implication is that if small business owners weren't so important to the economy, marketers wouldn't care about them.

Financial services firms are the worst offenders:

"We know how much small businesses contribute to the local economy. That's why you can count on us to understand the challenges you face today and do what we can to contribute to your future growth and profitability."
—Major United States bank

"Small business owners like you are vital to the Canadian economy. So we've designed . . ."
—Fortune 500 credit card company

They are absolutely right—collectively, the small business market is driving the growth of the economy. Individually, however, small business owners don't care.

Craftspeople are not hiring people and growing quickly, so they feel undeserving of such high praise. Freedom Fighters want to make their businesses run better and Mountain Climbers care about how you are going to help them double in sales this year.

Fixing the state of the country's economy is about 87th on their list of things to do today, and they're lucky if they get into double digits before sundown.

Maybe the fact that entrepreneurs don't think about their role in the national economy is a sad commentary about business owners. But I am more inclined to believe that they don't have time to think about tomorrow when they still have to worry about the other half of today. Regardless, they want to know how you can help them now.

In fact, rather than telling them they are important, prove it to them. American Express got it right with its campaign called *Voices from Main Street,* a program from American Express's Small Business Services that sought to champion the needs of small business leading up to the United States federal election in the year 2000. The program was so successful that American Express was the only commercial organization invited to testify before the House Subcommittee on Small Business about the hot-button issues that are facing entrepreneurs today.

So what was the secret behind *Voices'* success?

1. The program's idea itself is part of the reason for its success. From the start, *Voices* was more than a traditional ad campaign. Instead of talking about how important small business owners are to the economy in a patronizing tone, American Express focused on interacting with, listening to, and empowering the small business owner—in short, proving that they were important, not just saying it.

2. Redirecting part of the spend locally also contributed. The program combined above-the-line brand advertising, direct marketing and partnerships with live town-hall forums conducted on and offline. Reaching out to the entrepreneurial community at a local, grassroots level was crucial in engaging the audience and supporting the company's claim of being the true champions of small business.

I asked Peter Vaughn, Vice President and General Manager of American Express Small Business Services at the time, and the man behind the *Voices from Main Street* campaign, for his thoughts on the program: "We wanted to make the voice of the small business community louder, without taking sides on the political issues," explains Vaughn. "By championing the small business owners' interests, we were able to raise our overall visibility amongst cardmembers and potential customers."

Avoid talking about the role of small business in the national economy. Small business owners are worried about their own world and see this rhetoric as a transparent, disingenuous attempt to win them over. If you really want to show small business owners how important they are, prove it with actions, not words.

Show them (don't tell them) how important they are.

Selling a Seller

One of the fundamental differences between a consumer and a small business owner is their knowledge of, and experience in, sales.

The small business owner is a salesperson by definition. No matter how small a business or how untrained the owner, that owner must learn to sell and learn fast.

My wife Jennifer and I are Yin and Yang. They say opposites attract and I think we're living proof. We balance each other out well. While I dream up ideas, she analyzes them for their strengths and weaknesses. She's more detail oriented, whereas I'm a bit of a scatterbrain. I love to sell and Jennifer finds selling unnatural, even dirty.

But things are starting to change. Jennifer recently started a business from a spare bedroom in our home. She has only just dipped her toe into the world of entrepreneurship, but she has already started to talk about "prospects lists," "advancing the sale," and "closing." This is my wife!—the one who hates selling, talking about "closing."

Like all small business owners, Jennifer has had to start selling. No matter how reluctant they are to do so, almost all small business people have to sell their products or services. Even if they don't like it, the painter still has to sell the paint job, the jeweler has to find customers, and the mechanic must sell repair services. No matter how uncomfortable they are with the sales process in the beginning, they must sell to survive.

In fact, ask a handful of small business owners what sets them apart from people with a day job and they will tell you it is their ability and willingness to sell.

So when you develop your next campaign, imagine you are selling to a room full of salespeople. Don't try to put one over on them. They know that when you offer them a "chance to win," you really just want their names. They know what "while supplies last" really means, why you give them their first payment free, or why you're offering them all of those airline points.

They are savvy to the ways of the marketer because they do it every day. This does not mean that you have to stop marketing; just be honest. They respect your need to sell; it is one of the most significant things you have in common with them.

You're selling to a salesperson.

Street Credibility

So with such a tough group of salespeople on their hands, how are Fortune 500 marketers supposed to make their brands relevant to small business owners? You need to get *street credibility,* that elusive halo that can mean the difference between an entrepreneur's taking your company seriously or passing it by—and it is a very powerful force in the small business market.

Clare Loewenthal, publisher of Australia's leading small business publication *Dynamic Small Business Magazine* (DSB), explains why her magazine has street credibility with Australian small business owners:

> "I think the most fundamental reason for DSB's success is that the magazine is itself a small business. I understand the challenges facing our readers because I experience them every day," says Loewenthal. "Over the years, I have used my Publisher's Page to talk very personally about my own small business, and this seems to have built up incredible credibility and loyalty."

So, what if you work for a big company whose founder is a distant memory? It's tougher to get street credibility, but it is possible. One marketer targeting would-be entrepreneurs is Johnnie Walker Scotch Whiskey. Johnnie Walker recently launched the Keep Walking Fund, which provides cash grants of up to $500,000 to budding entrepreneurs. According to Bruce Winterton, Group Business Director for the Johnnie Walker account at Bartle Bogle Hegarty in New York, the campaign is targeted at men aged 25 to 34 who are "striving to succeed."

One of the creative components of the campaign is an "Entrepreneur's Survival Guide" insert that appeared in a number of business magazines, including *Business 2.0, Red Herring,* and *Industry Standard.*

This creative guide doesn't glamorize entrepreneurs in the way that many of the wanna-be entrepreneur magazines do with their get-rich-quick promises. Instead, it takes a humorous approach, offering tips on (among other things) choosing office space—namely, finding a place that offers "light, heat, and a low level of toxic fumes." It's a situation many small business owners can relate to and laugh at without feeling like they're being made fun of.

Says Winterton, "We tested this campaign with entrepreneurs and would-be entrepreneurs. We found that with the changing economy, in particular what's happened in the last 12 months, people were starving for a little entertainment and advice delivered in a tongue-in-cheek way."

The Keep Walking Fund made a key decision in its quest for credibility: they invited a board of directors composed of successful entrepreneurs who gave their stamp of approval to the campaign before agreeing to be on the board. Putting this advisory board in place gives Johnnie Walker the street credibility it needs to be able to talk about starting a business.

If you've got street credibility, flaunt it. If not, get it.

Sweating the Details

Ask a group of small business owners what frustrates them most about being in business for themselves, and more often than not they will tell you it's all the details—paperwork, forms—they have to manage. Running a business involves an enormous number of niggling little chores that larger businesses have created systems or job functions to manage: the lease needs to be reviewed, the payroll form needs to be filled in, the credit application for the new supplier needs to be completed.

Most small business owners have always resented every minute they waste on the details. Ask them what they were like as kids and they'll tell you they were restless, they couldn't sit still—some even had Attention Deficit Disorder (ADD). Today they can't stand waiting in lines and they have a very low tolerance for mundane, repetitive tasks. Mountain Climbers dislike details the most, but neither Freedom Fighters nor Craftspeople got into business for the paperwork.

I remember asking a new business owner named Steve about his goals. Steve explained that his definition of success was to grow to the point at which he could afford to hire an office manager to tend to the details of running a business. Steve's goal was not a revenue figure or a number on the bottom line; he just wanted someone else to sweat the details.

So when it comes to winning the hearts and wallets of business owners, ask yourself whether you are contributing to or taking away from their creative downtime. How long are your application forms? Do you prepopulate direct mail reply cards with name, address, and so on, so that the recipient need only sign it and send it back? Do they need to spend 10 minutes to register at your web site? Do you go to them, or do they have to come to you? Do your entrepreneurial clients get stuck playing telephone tag or is someone always there to help?

Free up a few minutes from the process of dealing with your company and you'll be rewarded by entrepreneurs trying to avoid mind-numbing minutiae.

Sweat the details for them.

Funny Business

Big companies often ask us whether it is acceptable to use humor when advertising to small business owners. The answer is most definitely yes! Small business owners have a sense of humor just like anyone else. Of course, there is a caveat— they should never be the butt of your joke.

One marketer who has effectively used humor to deliver a small business message is OmniSky, a wireless Internet and e-mail provider. OmniSky's ads describe how their technology will enable entrepreneurs to get out of the office and experience the phenomenon of a weekend; and just in case small business owners have forgotten what a weekend is, OmniSky defines it for them. Although the ad pokes fun at the dusk-to-dawn working mentality of entrepreneurs, it's done in a way that is tasteful and leaves the reader smiling with recognition.

I recently heard a radio ad for MYOB (Mind Your Own Business), a small business accounting software package, that got it wrong. The radio campaign features a woman business owner asking a sales clerk for an accounting program suitable for small business. When she learns she can save $100 on MYOB, she's ecstatic, gushing about how she can spend the extra money getting her roots done. This spot is an insult to women entrepreneurs, implying that the only reason women go into business for themselves is to earn some mad money to get their hair done.

Internet service provider MindSpring (now called Earthlink) ran an ad featuring a crying baby with the headline "Some website customers need their hands held. Heck, we'll even burp them and wipe their bottoms too" (see Figure 3.1). The obvious analogy between a business owner and a crybaby is not lost on the reader.

Using humor is great—small business owners could use a good laugh. Just make sure that you laugh with them, not at them.

Laugh with, not at your target audience.

Just Did It

Our company recently took a poll of 500 students interested in starting a business. We asked, "What is the biggest obstacle

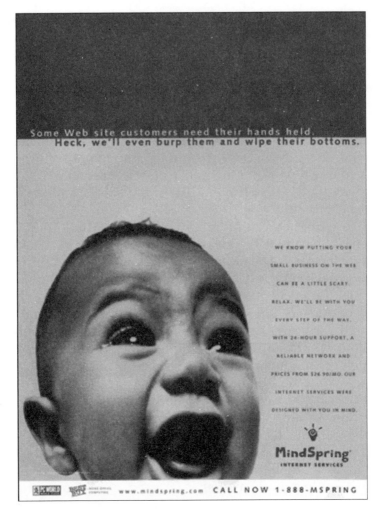

Figure 3.1

Source: © 2001 EarthLink, Inc. MindSpring is a trademark of EarthLink, Inc. This has been reprinted with the express written permission of EarthLink, Inc.

stopping you from starting your business?" Seventy percent replied that it was access to capital.

Balderdash!

Consider this: in 2000, 42 percent of Inc. 500 companies (the magazine's annual survey of the fastest-growing companies in the United States) were started for less than $10,000.[2]

Additionally, the students we surveyed are graduating in arguably the most entrepreneur-friendly time in history. Various levels of government are making additional money available to young businesspeople. Combined with various bank-led initiatives, getting $20,000 to start a business has never been easier.

The difference between a business owner and the rest of the world is that entrepreneurs act on their ideas. They take the initiative and accept the risk. While others analyze, ponder, and pontificate, small business owners act. It is in their nature to take action while others evaluate.

You're talking to doers.

The Indiana Jones of the Business World?

The media are quick to portray entrepreneurs as risk takers willing to put it all on the line for the promise of big rewards. They perpetuate the stereotype of entrepreneurs as people who throw caution to the winds to market products everybody told them would never fly, adventurers swinging from one life-threatening predicament to the next. But do entrepreneurs consider themselves risk takers?

Yes and no.

Business owners acknowledge that an inherent risk accompanies what they do. But they accept it as a necessary trade-off for greater rewards such as freedom and financial gain. Many entrepreneurs tell me that in fact, working for someone else is much riskier than being an entrepreneur. They argue that business owners control their own destinies, whereas salaried workers are at the whim of their managers and could be let go for no reason other than to buoy the stock price.

So be careful referring to small business owners as risk

2. The Inc. 500 Almanac, op. cit.

takers. To be sure, Mountain Climbers are most comfortable with risk, Freedom Fighters are somewhat less comfortable with it, while Craftspeople are the least comfortable with risk. But the one thing all three have in common is that they attempt to minimize and manage risk rather than savor it.

Business owners accept risk; they don't seek it.

Your Mother Told You Never to Ask This

Most companies that build a database of small business customers and prospects want to capture information about each firm's annual revenue in an attempt to segment by size of business. This may be a tasty piece of information for you to know, but asking small business owners about their gross revenue is the equivalent of asking acquaintances how much money they earn or how they vote. Unless you have the kind of relationship that requires you to know, asking is rude at best. At worst, it could detract from the relationship you are building with your customers.

I can remember one of our clients was trying to sign up small business owners for a new loyalty program the company had just launched. This client wanted to know the size of the companies that were signing up for the program because our client could then sell that information to the loyalty program's partners. The company asked applicants to reveal their companys' annual revenue upon signing up for the program. Just 30 percent of the applicants chose to answer this question. The other 70 percent clearly felt it was none of our client's business.

Why are small business owners so sensitive about gross revenue? Because it is the yardstick by which they measure themselves. Used as a criterion for the Inc. 500 and the PROFIT 100, a minimum gross revenue is also a membership requirement for the Young Entrepreneurs' Organization and the Young Presidents' Organization.

Instead of asking about gross revenue, ask small business owners how many employees they have. Number of employees is a much less sensitive question and can act as a proxy for gross revenue in a pinch. Here's how it works: If you really need to know a small business's gross revenue, estimate it by using the rough guide of $100,000 in revenue per employee. So for instance, if a small business has 10 employees, it is likely doing about a million dollars in annual sales.

This is by no means an exact formula and depends on how capital-intensive the industry is; manufacturing companies typically have a high gross revenue per employee and service-based businesses often have less. However, the $100,000 figure is a general guideline that allows you to determine the size of the company you are profiling without offending.

Mind your Ps and Qs.

Hiring Headaches

One of the biggest challenges business owners face is people-related issues. New companies rarely have a brand name they can use to attract the best talent. Their benefit plans are often weak or nonexistent compared to those of the Fortune 500. In fact, a 2000 study conducted by George S. May International Co. revealed that 74 percent of small business owners feel that finding employees is their toughest management challenge.[3]

Some small business marketers are now getting to small business owners' wallets by trying to solve one of their biggest headaches. MasterCard is running an ad campaign that features a group of attractive young people hanging out (see Figure 3.2). The headline reads:

- $3,000 of comfy office furniture: $1,920
- $7,000 of new computer equipment & software: $6,600
- $4,000 staff retreat: $3,500

3. George S. May International Co, *The May International Survey,* October, 2000.

Figure 3.2
Source: Courtesy of MasterCard

- Creating a place where people want to show up at 9 a.m.: priceless

Chevrolet is getting into the game, too (see Figure 3.3). Its ad for the Chevy Express truck starts off with the owner of a construction company saying, "My mechanics love them. My

"My mechanics love them.
My guys aren't grouchy. You should have seen them
before we switched to Chevy."

~ *Mike Vargo, D&K Construction*

"We do construction and maintenance. Drug stores. Supermarkets. We're always on call, so our vans are critical

to our business. My guys just love the Chevy Express! I mean the thing rides like a car. Really nice. And the bin

package with its lockable doors for tools even got them organized. So

we reached a turning point when we went completely to Chevy."

(For more info, call 1-800-950-2438 or visit www.chevrolet.com.)

Chevy. The most dependable, longest-lasting trucks on the road.

CHEVY EXPRESS ⟨⟨⟨ **LIKE A ROCK**

Figure 3.3
Source: Courtesy of General Motors Corporation

guys aren't grouchy. You should have seen them before we switched to Chevy."

Never underestimate the importance a business owner places in keeping the staff happy.

The way to their wallet may be through their team.

The Intrapreneurs

When you market to small business owners, don't overlook the influence of the people who work for them.

As a small business grows, the number of people involved in choosing suppliers grows, too. First the little choices (like which courier company to use), then the bigger decisions (like choosing a technology supplier) eventually fall into the hands of front-line workers.

I remember sitting down to meet with a group of customers from an office-supply retailer. This company had invested handsomely to build psychographic models to understand the ways small business owners think and their attitudes towards growth. Soon after the conversation began, it became clear that the customers who were buying our client's products were not the business owners the company had so desperately attempted to understand; rather, the retailer's best customers were office managers and receptionists at the targeted small businesses. This retailer had spent an enormous amount of time and money trying to understand the company owner's attitudes and idiosyncrasies, but this information was worthless because somebody else was making the buying decisions.

Buying office supplies is one of the first responsibilities small business owners delegate to others. These marketers were busy trying to understand the owners when they should have been cozying up to the office managers.

And people who work for small businesses buy differently from their big business counterparts. Workers in small businesses feel like they are actually making a difference. As a result, workers in small businesses tend to be happier and more loyal than those in any other types of organizations. Consider the employee satisfaction chart in Figure 3.4. Employees in small businesses are more satisfied than are their counterparts in medium- and large-sized businesses.[4]

4. The 1997 Inc./Gallup Survey, "The State of the American Workforce," *Inc. Magazine* 19, no. 7 (15 May 1997).

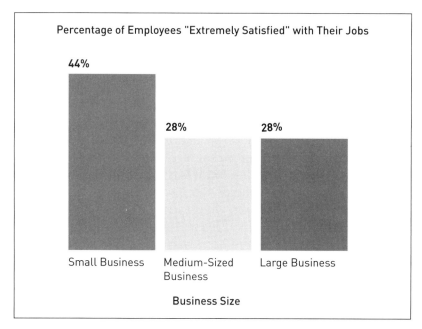

Figure 3.4 Employees Satisfaction Figures by Business Size

Source: The 1997 Inc./Gallup Survey, "The State of the American Workforce," *Inc. Magazine* 19, no. 07 (15 May 1997).

Gallup reports that when small business employees were asked if their company does what it takes to make a great working environment, 82 percent agreed, whereas only 70 percent of employees from larger organizations agreed.[5]

Small business workers are more devoted despite lower wages, inferior health plans, and older equipment. Often, small business workers enjoy greater autonomy, a chance to work on a broader range of tasks, and a sense of accomplishment.

Less obvious (but no less important) is the closeness employees feel to the owner both physically and emotionally.

5. The 1996 Inc./ Gallup Survey, "The Happiest Workers In The World," *Inc. Magazine* 18, no. 7 (15 May 1996).

Unlike the faceless corporation in which shareholders are invisible and represented only by board members whom the average employee never meets, small business workers see their shareholder(s) every morning and consequently feel a greater sense of duty.

Finally, from a practical standpoint, small business employees know their companies have fewer resources than a large business; thus they often feel they have to perform or their company, and therefore their job, may be in danger.

So when you market to small business, think of the company as more than just the owner. Behind the scenes may be a team of *intrapreneurs* who will be less likely to choose a supplier for personal or political reasons and more likely to select a vendor that's good for the home team.

Think beyond the owner.

Don't Throw the Brand Out with the Bath Water

Small business owners think most Fortune 500 companies are big, slow, and expensive. As a result, many big companies toy with the idea of adopting a separate brand for the small business division. It can work, but this tactic should be used only as a last resort because a creating a separate small business brand comes with a huge price tag.

One company that tried—and ultimately failed—to create a stand-alone small business brand from scratch was PrimeStreet.com. PrimeStreet.com was a financial services player that promised small business owners competing bids on their borrowing needs. The company attempted to drive small business owners to its web site through mass advertising but failed to lower costs enough for the method to be sustainable. Then the company abandoned its attempt to create a brand in the small business market and tried to sell its tool to other banks for use on their sites. Nevertheless, the solution proved to be too little too late; PrimeSteet.com closed its doors in early 2001 after failing to receive a third round of financing.

Before shutting down the business, I had a chance to talk to then-CEO of PrimeStreet.com, Kevin Talbot. Talbot had some clear advice for anyone attempting to create a small business brand from scratch: "I think any company that wants to create brand awareness in the small business marketplace should seriously consider how much money is really required," says Talbot. "In our view, it takes more time and more money than you expect in order to build enough brand identity to create brand awareness within the target market. It is an ongoing process that needs to be continually reinforced and even then, you are not guaranteed you will gain sustainable mind share."

If you are lucky enough to have a Fortune 500 brand at your disposal, consider what Pitney Bowes did to shed its brand baggage in the small business space. Pitney Bowes launched PitneyWorks as a quasi-independent company focused on the needs of small business. You can tell from the company's name that it is affiliated with a trustworthy company, but the *Works* suffix holds a promise of something new and more relevant.

However tempting a brand dedicated to small business is, think twice. It is much cheaper to make a trustworthy old brand seem more entrepreneurial than it is to start from scratch.

Make your existing brand relevant.

Step #4: Find a Simulator

Now that you have segmented the small business market into homogeneous chunks,
found your aggregator, and are speaking
their language, you've got customers—congratulations. Your
final challenge is to figure out a way to keep them happy.

That's easy, you say, we can give them a web site where
they can place orders, and we can communicate with direct
mail so that we don't have the cost of a sales force. The problem, however, is that small business owners are obsessed with
customer service.

What would keep you coming back to the family-owned
hardware store down the street rather than going to one of
the hardware mega-stores? How can a corner hardware store
compete when its selection and buying power are dwarfed by
the might of the superstores? The answer is customer service.

Small business owners offer their customers impeccable
customer service and will go to practically any lengths to keep
a customer. They in turn expect the same of you. They want
one-on-one account management in which the sales representative goes to them.

Because most companies cannot afford to service the
small business market with account managers, they look for

ways to take costs out of their delivery channel. They usually attempt to make the relationship as low touch as possible—exactly the opposite of what small business owners give their own customers and expect of you.

To solve this difficulty, marketers need to simulate a high-touch experience without actually incurring the expense of offering it.

As the examples in the coming pages demonstrate, simulators are often enabled by some form of technology (defined broadly to include call centers, direct mail, and the Internet). But for a simulator to truly replace an account manager, you must realize that by forcing them to deal with you through some sort of technologically enabled simulator, you take something away from the relationship—a live person. In return, and to tip the scales in your favor, you need to offer a service benefit that exceeds even what a live person could do.

Find an intelligent simulator.

Hook Up the IV

One way to simulate the experience of a one-on-one account-managed relationship is to put your relationship with entrepreneurs on autopilot. Seth Godin called this method *intravenous marketing* in his pioneering book *Permission Marketing*. The concept is simple: build your relationship with customers so that they trust you enough to give them what they need without ever having to order it (much like you trust a doctor to administer the correct dosage of medicine when you're hooked up to an IV; hence the name intravenous marketing).

This servicing technique is particularly achievable for small business marketers for two reasons:

1. Most small business owners are overwhelmed by details; they are only too glad to delegate mindless ordering tasks.
2. Small businesses often lack support help; conse-

quently, ordering basic supplies often falls onto the already full to-do list of the owner.

Merrill Lynch has done a nice job of intravenous marketing in the small business sector. The folks at Merrill started to court small business owners when they realized that 70 percent of the wealthy customers they targeted—those with five million dollars or more in assets—were small business owners. They researched the market and found most business owners to be terrible personal money managers. The business owners typically devoted a disproportionate amount of time to managing their businesses' finances, and their personal finances were a mess.

So Merrill Lynch found a way to put the servicing of small business owners on autopilot. Its so-called sweep account automatically transfers excess fund balances from a designated bank account to a better-performing Merrill Lynch investment account. The key to the account is that small business owners don't have to ask for the transaction; it happens automatically when the balance in the designated account hits a predetermined point set by the owner. In May 2000, *Business Week* magazine reported that the Merrill Lynch sweep account grew from $50 billion in assets to more than $150 billion between 1996 and 1999.[1]

Other suppliers that do a good job of intravenous marketing in the small business sector are the bottled-water companies. At Warrillow & Co. we have 20 people on staff. A few years ago, a staff member suggested we purchase a water cooler. Because our staff included only three people at the time, a water cooler seemed a little excessive; I went along with the idea, however, because it did not pose a significant expense. I gave the water cooler company my credit card number and they promptly delivered a dispenser and two bottles of water. At the time it seemed as though the two huge containers of water would last us for months, but the people

1. Heather Timmons, "For Merrill, Small is Bountiful," *Business Week*, 22 May 2000.

from the water company said they would be back to check in with us from time to time to see if we needed more water. If we did, they explained, they would just put the cost of the refill on my card.

That was three years ago and since then I have never had to think about the water cooler in our office. There is always just enough water for us and never so much that it is a hassle to store. Part of the supplier's secret is employing friendly drivers who get to know the office staff. We have moved offices three times within the building; each time the water cooler company's driver found out about our move from someone in our office so that I didn't need to waste time letting the water company know.

Another benefit of intravenous marketing in the small business sector is how incredibly loyal and dependent entrepreneurs are to autopilot service. At our office we go through a bottle of water per week and our supply is restocked without our ever having to ask for it. They've got us for life! With all of the things going on in our little company, ordering water would never make it to the to-do list. With all of the expenses to renegotiate, a weekly $15 bottle of water would probably never make the list of suppliers we consider renegotiating with. By replenishing our supply automatically, they continue to make money from us without our really noticing. The only way we would consider looking at other vendors is if they got the dosage wrong. In other words, if we started running out of water, we would be forced to call for more; that would diminish our loyalty significantly.

Servicing the small business market through a traditional sales force (the kind that calls prospects to make an appointment and according to many sales organizations costs an average of about $400 per sales call) is usually prohibitively expensive. If you consider that disadvantage along with the fact that entrepreneurs hate details and usually lack administrative support, you can probably justify trying to hook up an IV to your small business customer base.

Do your small business customers trust you to administer the correct dosage?

Slaves to Service

Once you have found your simulator, you need to institution-alize, reward, and recognize customer service wherever a small business owner touches your simulator. It sounds trite, but one of the secrets to winning the small business market is ensuring that, however you simulate one-to-one service, you fortify your customer service capabilities. Investing in your servicing capabilities is simply a cost of entry you must be willing to pay, or your other efforts will be pointless.

An hour before their flights, small business travelers who deal with biztravel.com get a message (called a bizAlert) sent to their pagers, providing them with gate information and updates on any delays or cancellations. Frequent-flying entre-preneurs can also download their itineraries to their pre-ferred mobile device, thanks to another biztravel innovation called CalendarDirect.

Dell offers a unique tracking service for deliveries, as well as an online service that allows the small business owner to type in a computer's service tag number and find out how much additional memory the computer needs in order to ac-commodate a particular program. Dell even has a Customer Experience Council that continually monitors the entire cus-tomer experience from the time of purchase to receipt of de-livery.

American Express has won the hearts and wallets of small business owners because the company almost always takes the cardmembers' word for it when a dispute arises about a purchase. The company's policy is to remove the charge from the cardmember's statement first and then follow up with the merchant. This policy results in a perception of a very customer-centered organization.

Small business owners already know that they wear the customer service crown. If you can approach their level of cus-tomer service, however, and then impress them with your own competitive advantages like product selection and pricing, you can soften even the toughest small business customer.

Small business owners think your service stinks.

Face Time

Would you like to see whether your customer service is keeping small business owners loyal or driving them away? Get into the trenches with them. See where they work and understand their frustrations.

A number of companies do this well: In 2001 the people at Intuit launched a program in which executives shadow entrepreneurs for a day. American Express brings its team together with small business owners over lunch at customer appreciation days. And at UPS, managers have to spend time actually driving the delivery truck—a fantastic way to gain understanding about what's going on at the customer level.

If driving trucks doesn't appeal to you, consider developing your own small business advisory council or learning panel. Regular interaction with a cache of real-life entrepreneurs can provide a sounding board for your small business programs, as well as give you some face time with your prospects.

Walk a mile in their shoes.

Retail Is Not Dead after All

First, catalog shopping was supposed to kill retail; then the Internet threatened to deal the final blow. Well, video did not kill the radio star, nor did toll-free numbers and URLs (uniform resource locators) kill the importance of the retail channel for simulating one-on-one account management in the small business market.

Whether your idea of a branch is a kiosk in an airport or a big box store, small businesses like dealing with real people. Furthermore, in the absence of being able to send an account manager to them, having an account manager on hand in a retail store is often the best alternative. Consider the following:

- *Small Business Banker* magazine surveyed small business owners and found that retail is the channel of choice for 71 percent of entrepreneurs.[2]
- In 2000, Gateway—a pioneer in phone and web sales of computer hardware—actually started to build branches to service small business customers.
- In the spring of 2001, Staples bought back shares in its staples.com experiment, bringing the formerly stand-alone company back under the corporate wing of its parent. It seems that selling office supplies on-line did not warrant a unique legal entity and that the Staples retail stores would continue to be the company's most important channel.

Retail is an expensive way to service the small business market. Depending on your industry, however, it may be the most cost-effective way to give small business owners a live person to contact.

Retail is not dead in the small business market.

Simulating Loyalty

Think for a moment about your favorite account representative from a supplier of yours. Chances are that near or at the top of the list of attributes you like about this individual is that he or she understands and appreciates your business.

One of the greatest ways to offer these desirable attributes of good account management in the small business market is to simulate them through the effective use of a loyalty program. Loyalty programs simulate the ideal account manager because they are typically based on some knowledge management system designed to understand its members. The other element of most loyalty programs is some sort of cur-

2. Small Business Banker, "Branches Hang Tough!" *Small Business Banker* 2, no. 4 (April 2001): 25.

rency or benefit that allows companies to show their appreciation.

And small business owners love loyalty programs, one of the great tax loopholes left for entrepreneurs. Small business owners sit in a kind of no-man's-land where they can use the spending power of their businesses to earn points much faster than most consumers. In addition, most small businesses are not large enough to qualify for formalized corporate discount/loyalty programs that typically benefit the business with better rates and formal procurement systems, instead of airline points and a catalogue of gifts that benefit the owner.

As a result, most credit card spending is put through on an owner's account and the owner uses all of those points as a tax-free perk (although some countries make small business owners claim points as a taxable benefit, very few entrepreneurs actually do). They redeem points for family trips and gifts they would never buy with after-tax dollars.

In a study our company conducted about small business loyalty programs, we found that almost 80 percent of small business owners who were members of at least one loyalty program said that they designate a portion of their loyalty program rewards for personal use.[3] Only 14.4 percent use their rewards strictly for business (see Figure 4.1).

To further research why points are accumulated, we asked small business owners who are members of one or more loyalty programs and use their rewards exclusively to benefit their businesses whether they parlay their points into rewarding employees.

A mere 5.5 percent of the small business owners we surveyed said that they use their loyalty program points to reward their staff (see Figure 4.2).

When it comes to points, small business owners are not using them to motivate and reward key employees—they love

3. Warrillow & Co., "The Impact of Loyalty Programs on the Buying Behaviors of Small Business Owners," *Warrillow Report* 01, no. 04.

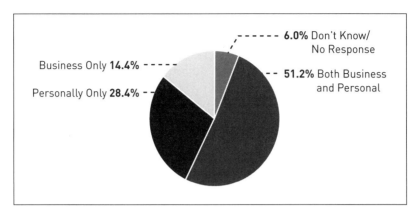

Figure 4.1 How Entrepreneurs Allocate Loyalty Program
Reward Points

Source: Warrillow & Co., "The Impact of Loyalty Programs on the Buying Behaviors of Small
Business Owners," *Warrillow Report,* Issue 04, Vol.01, Toronto, 2000.

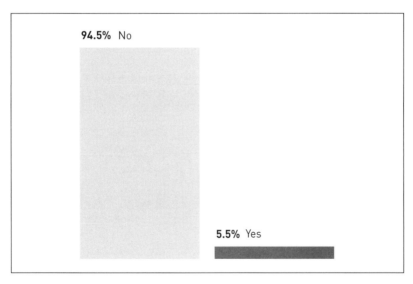

Figure 4.2 Percentage of Small Business Owners Who Use
Points to Reward Employees

Source: Warrillow & Co., "The Impact of Loyalty Programs on the Buying Behaviors of Small
Business Owners," *Warrillow Report,* Issue 04, Vol.01.

their points too much and see them as one of the great perks of being the boss.

Think of loyalty programs as an effective way to simulate the experience of one-on-one account management. Structure your program as you would an account-managed relationship: get to know the customer, understand the customer's needs, and reward loyalty with perks and extras.

Let them collect for business and travel for pleasure.

Show Them the Money

If you still want further proof that entrepreneurs love their points, consider this: in the same study, we asked small business owners who are members of one or more loyalty programs how they would improve those programs.

Their choice was quite clear (see Figure 4.3). Sixty-four percent said they would increase the rewards or discounts,

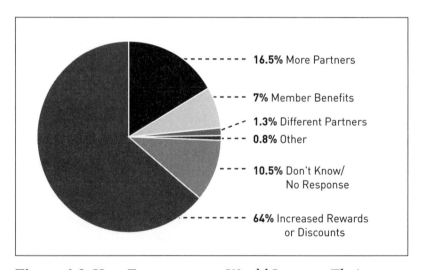

Figure 4.3 How Entrepreneurs Would Improve Their Preferred Loyalty Program

Source: Warrillow & Co., "The Impact of Loyalty Programs on the Buying Behaviors of Small Business Owners," *Warrillow Report*, Issue 04, Vol.01.

and only 16.5 percent of the small business owners we surveyed said they would like to see more sponsors signed up.

It was also revealed that 51.5 percent of these small business owners would pay a $50 annual fee to accelerate their program points or discounts. So rather than adding more partners or extra benefits to your loyalty program to entice small business owners further, you are better off appealing to their passion for points.

You do not have to be an airline or credit card company to use loyalty programs to simulate account management in the small business market. Both Sprint and AT&T have experimented with loyalty programs for their small business customers. Chase Manhattan Bank has offered Continental airline points in return for a business owner's opening a deposit account.

Business owners love their points.

Too Much of a Good Thing?

The effectiveness and popularity of loyalty programs have not been lost on small business marketers. In fact, practically every category—from rental cars to telecommunications—that sells to entrepreneurs offers some type of small business loyalty program; if small business owners buy a product or service, you can bet they will be offered membership in a loyalty program.

Not surprisingly, of the 400 small business owners we interviewed for our loyalty program study (they had to be a member of at least one loyalty program to participate in the study), more than 60 percent of entrepreneurs belong to more than one program and almost 20 percent belong to four programs or more (see Figure 4.4).

If so many entrepreneurs are members of more than one program already, does the world need yet another small business loyalty program? Maybe. Before you launch your own, however, seriously consider joining an existing coalition program. These programs join together a group of companies

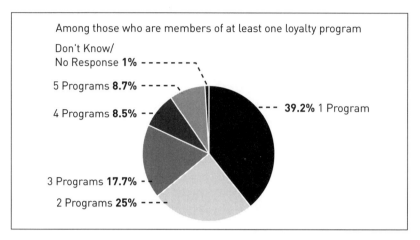

Among those who are members of at least one loyalty program

Don't Know/
No Response **1%**

5 Programs **8.7%**

4 Programs **8.5%**

39.2% 1 Program

3 Programs **17.7%**

2 Programs **25%**

Figure 4.4 Number of Loyalty Programs to Which
Entrepreneurs Belong
Source: Warrillow & Co., "The Impact of Loyalty Programs on the Buying Behaviors of Small
Business Owners," *Warrillow Report,* Issue 04, Vol.01, Toronto, 2000.

that share a common desire to reach small business owners.
Each sponsor company agrees to a certain level of cross-
selling and information sharing.

Coalition programs have the added benefit of being acquisition tools as well as retention methods. When we asked
Fortune 500 companies what they liked best about being a
member of a coalition loyalty program, they cited the ability
to cross-sell to other coalition members' customers as their
favorite part of their loyalty program arrangement.

The small business market may not need another loy-
alty program.

Why Small Business Chat Rooms Don't Work

Another tactic used to compensate for a lack of one-on-one
account management in the small business market is the creation of chat rooms on the web site of Fortune 500 small busi-

ness marketers. I cannot count the number of times I have been in a meeting with a Fortune 500 marketing team and they suggest "building a community" of small business owners at their web site to create a loyal customer base. The theory usually goes something like this: "We'll build a community; small business owners will come to our site to solve problems and get answers from their fellow entrepreneurs. We'll benefit from being the host of this little party in terms of stickier, more loyal clients." The theory sounds magical. In reality, creating a chat room and community at your web site to keep customers loyal almost never works for three reasons:

1. Lack of credibility: A Fortune 500 company lacks credibility hosting a community of small business owners. Why would small business owners gather at a bank's or a credit card company's web site when they can visit sites that offer advice as their core business and not just as a quaint loyalty ploy?

2. Lack of independence: When small business owners can meet anywhere on the web, why would they form a community at a site that clearly has an agenda?

3. Lack of a common theme: All good communities are built around what members have in common. As mentioned throughout this book, small business owners identify more with fellow members of an industry and see little in common with the rest of the small business community. If they were to join a community, it would be made up of people in the same industry.

Carmine Porco, a Managing Partner of an Internet Business Solutions Group for Cisco Systems, advises that small business marketers talk to their customers first before developing any online initiative: "We were building a small business site for a large bank and tried to predict what small business owners would want to see. We did focus groups and learned a great deal. Some of it was surprising, but provided good insight into the market. We assumed they'd want chat sessions to converse with lawyers and get advice, or software that would allow them to do their books online. What we learned is that they were looking for more simple, straight-forward capabilities, like the ability to pay bills online. They told us they had their own communities, they had their own lawyers, and they didn't want to chat."

Not convinced? Visit the community section of any Fortune 500 marketer and view the archived chats. You will find a measly trickle of two or three entries per week. Consider two or three business owners as a percentage of their small business customer base and you will see just how few business owners care about chat rooms.

Unless your mainline business is advice, do not try to build a community of small business owners at your web site—it won't work.

Leave the communities to someone else.

Breaking the Barriers to Doing Business Online

In the late nineties, most of our Fortune 500 clients were investing heavily in building web sites. They believed that the Internet would allow them to service small business owners online, drastically reducing their costs of keeping small business customers happy. The Internet offered Fortune 500 companies the best shot at truly simulating the experience of one-on-one account management. The problem was that small business owners did not flock to the web to make their transactions, and (with a few exceptions) most sites were a major disappointment for their sponsors.

So in early 2001 we conducted research in order to understand why small business owners were not buying online. We interviewed entrepreneurs who had purchased online using credit cards to ensure that our research would not be monopolized by a discussion about security. Security is a legitimate concern of entrepreneurs, but we wanted to see beyond that issue to uncover the other factors that stop entrepreneurs from conducting more transactions via the Internet.

Through our research, we found five main barriers stopping small business owners from buying online. We call the first barrier the *expertise factor.*

Most small business owners tend to be generalists with a working knowledge of a wide variety of subjects. They don't have time to be experts in any one area; consequently, when they need to purchase products that are right for their business, they rely on the expertise and personalized advice of sales professionals. Small business owners use Value-Added Resellers (VARs) for their technology decisions or business banking professionals to handle their financial questions.

What small business owners find lacking in the do-it-yourself experience of transacting online is their suppliers' expertise on which they rely. As one entrepreneur told us, "The web gives me 10,000 years' worth of information, but zero experience and zero advice."

You can overcome the expertise factor in a number of ways. First, you can offer an online diagnostic tool that helps small business owners find the product that best suits their needs. American Express offers a "CardFinder for Business," which is a quick online survey designed to point users toward selecting the right card for them. The tool asks the user a series of questions and then makes a recommendation based on the answers. CardFinder simulates the experience of consulting with a good account representative who would ask a variety of questions, get to know the customer's business, and make an intelligent recommendation based on that customer's particular business situation.

You can also make it easier for them to get in touch with you, with instant messaging or with a prominently placed toll-free number on every page of your web site. By integrating these types of features into your web site, you will stand a better chance of attracting small business owners to deal with you online.

Make self-service seem like full-service.

The Anonymity Syndrome

We called the second barrier stopping small business owners from dealing with suppliers online the *anonymity syndrome.* Price-sensitive small business owners are used to being able to negotiate a deal on almost anything—and most will tell you that they are quite proud of this skill. However, when it comes to buying online, the anonymity of the Internet and lack of flexibility to bargain for a lower price or a quicker turnaround time are features they find frustrating.

The entrepreneurs we studied told us that they value their personal supplier relationships because they enable the entrepreneurs to negotiate price discounts and better shipping dates. As one of our focus group attendees stated, "My rep gives me a price break on big jobs and can give me faster turnaround when I need it."

Other business owners regaled us with stories of how they were able to negotiate better terms, more credit, or better product availability through the power of their personalities. Business owners generally are confident people and pride themselves in being able to trump the system and negotiate smarter than the average Joe. In fact, many business owners say that paying full price for anything is a sure sign of entrepreneurial incompetence.

Federal Express gets beyond the anonymity syndrome in an innovative way. Traditionally, FedEx has offered volume shipping discounts to their business customers. These deals traditionally have been struck during a personal visit from a FedEx account representative. FedEx then embeds the discount negotiated in the offline world into the DNA of the customer's account number. Then when the small business enters its account number online, the deal negotiated in the offline world is automatically recognized in the online world. It's a great example of a system that allows entrepreneurs to deal in an offline world while maximizing the advantages of servicing them online.

The anonymity of buying online is unnatural for entrepreneurs.

The Cobweb Syndrome

The third barrier that keeps small business owners from buying from your web site is called the *cobweb syndrome*. The entrepreneurs we interviewed felt that big company web sites are not updated on a regular basis and do not necessarily reflect current pricing or product lines. As a result, they tend to rely on in-store visits to ensure that they see the latest models at the best sale prices.

One entrepreneur in our study captured this phenomenon: "I always check my Saturday paper for the best deals. You don't get those deals online." This may not actually hold true for your web site—but it is the perception small business owners have about shopping online for their businesses. Ironic, isn't it? The Internet has allowed big companies to provide up-to-the-minute information to its small business customers, yet in the minds of entrepreneurs, it's old news!

How then do you clear out these perceived cobwebs? Delta Hotels aggressively targets the small business market and gets around the cobweb syndrome by posting the day's date prominently on the company's home page. The web site also provides a changing "Rates and Availability" link that assures skeptical business shoppers that the prices they see online are current and updated, and that the hotel room they are seeking is currently available.

Also take advantage of offline vehicles to help promote your newest online offerings. Because many small business owners think locally and look for sales and specials in their Saturday metro newspaper, you can insert a flyer or an advertisement announcing upcoming online deals. Finally, to really cement your web site's reputation for providing up-to-the-minute information, consider giving online purchasers a one-day sale advantage over retail shoppers.

Make your site local.

145

The See, Touch, and Feel Factor

We named the fourth barrier to online purchasing the *see, touch, and feel factor,* which in particular pertains to high-priced items such as office furniture, computers, and wireless systems. When it comes to big purchases, entrepreneurs often use the Internet as a research tool and then test products in the store. Their need to see whether that new chair will suit a trick back or whether that funky new cell phone model will fit comfortably into an overcoat pocket goes beyond the obvious: large purchases represent a proportionately greater investment of time and money for small businesses than they do for large corporations. When an executive at a large company needs a new computer, he or she sends a message to the purchasing department. The individual in purchasing is paid to spend time investigating what product will best meet the executive's needs, negotiating a price, and setting a delivery date. If the new computer turns out to be a bad investment and must be replaced, the executive can temporarily make use of the system of a vacationing employee or a computer sitting in an empty cubicle. The executive has no personal financial interest and very little time invested in the entire transaction.

Buying or replacing a high-ticket item like a computer is much different at a small company. Because most small businesses lack a purchasing department, time-consuming purchase decisions must be made by the business owner or by a trusted employee. Cost is of greater importance because the money invested in the product is largely the business owner's. If the new product does not meet the employee's needs, the company's productivity is directly impacted because spare computers are rarely available for use. One business owner told us:

> "My staff and I don't have time to run around and figure out why the computer we bought isn't doing this or isn't connecting with that, and we don't have time for it to be breaking down."

For some companies, overcoming the see, touch, and feel factor is as simple as minimizing the risk of a bad investment. Teligent, a Virginia-based communications company, prominently displays their no-risk guarantee from each of their product description pages. The guarantee reads: "If you're not completely satisfied with Teligent's local or long distance service for any reason, we'll pay to reconnect you to your old service provider." Entrepreneurs are thus reassured that the decision to choose an unknown or unproven supplier, even for a service as critical as telecommunications, will not have costly repercussions.

Make the online purchase as low risk as possible.

The Relationship Security Blanket

I once spoke to a management consultant who runs her own firm specializing in mergers and acquisitions. Despite having administrative staff who handle the business's day-to-day financing, she makes a point of going into the bank personally once every month or so. Every time she goes, she brings her account manager that day's edition of the local newspaper.

"Why do you do that?" I asked.

"Well," she replied, "you wouldn't believe how many times it's gotten me out of NSF (nonsufficient funds) checks!"

No matter how sophisticated and technically savvy small business owners become, many still want an account-managed relationship with their suppliers. Small business owners who use Internet banking will tell you that they love it for the convenience it provides, but they generally use the Internet for simple, day-to-day transactions, such as paying bills, checking bank balances, and viewing lists of cleared checks. Most maintain personal relationships with their banks in case they need to request a favor or investigate a transaction gone wrong.

Furthermore, it's not just their bank manager relationship that entrepreneurs value. Small business owners foster relationships with as many of their important suppliers as possible. They use these relationships as a safety net in case they get into trouble and need a rush order or have to defer a payment temporarily until a receivable comes in. Because they do not make the volume purchases that large corporations do, small business owners must count on strength of personality and an ability to create relationships with suppliers to gain leverage that they need. Maintaining a personal relationship with suppliers makes entrepreneurs feel as though they have someone to call if they are in trouble.

As technology improves, marketers are finding ways to minimize the relationship security blanket by simulating a personal relationship online. Wells Fargo, a bank known for its success in the small business market, simulates a personal relationship with small business customers through the Resource Center for Small Business. Users receive a personalized greeting ("Hello, Joe") as well as a customized home page that features information on stocks that they follow and their financial planning tools of choice, as well as their purchase history and personalized bookmarks. All of these features are customized to create the impression that Wells Fargo actually knows Joe personally.

This idea of personalizing the online experience can be taken a step further by asking regular small business customers to answer a new question about their businesses every few online visits. Entrepreneurs like being asked about their businesses, and having information about their unique selling proposition and their biggest business challenge can help small business marketers create targeted up-sell promotions. ***Simulate the account-managed relationship online.***

CHAPTER 5

Conclusion

Your Four-Step Action Plan

t's time to get started. You have four big challenges between you and the most important market on earth. Solve each challenge step by step:

Step 1: Forget about the small business market. It does not really exist. It is composed of a number of submarkets; therefore, your first task is to segment your customer base into buckets. Put your most profitable customers in bucket A, your next most profitable customers in bucket B, and so on. Then analyze your buckets to find a commonality that binds each bucket together. It could be a demographic trait like a geographic region, a firmographic characteristic like number of employees, or a psychographic trait. Most likely, a combination of a variety of traits is what makes each bucket unique. When you understand your buckets, you will be in a position to go out and acquire more customers like your most profitable ones.

Step 2: Find an aggregator. Because the small business market is so fragmented, your traditional media buy needs to be supplemented with an aggregator. Find out where your bucket A customers gather naturally. The best aggregators are physical, but you may also consider a vertical or horizontal association or a place where small business owners gather virtually.

Step 3: Speak their language. With such a fragmented market, no magic formula guarantees successful communication with small business owners. However, you need to learn a few general guidelines in order to avoid a land mine when you communicate with entrepreneurs.

Step 4: Find a simulator. Small business owners see customer service as their lifeblood. As a result, they raise the bar for the customer service they expect of you. Individually, however, small business owners rarely underwrite the cost of the one-on-one account-managed relationship that they so desperately want. Your challenge, therefore, is to find a way to simulate that one-on-one, high-touch experience at a cost that is sustainable.

Remember, today more businesses will be born in the United States than babies. Go now and claim your piece of the small business market.

An Invitation

Please keep in touch by joining our community of Fortune 500 marketers interested in reaching the small business sector. By subscribing to *Warrillow Weekly*, you will receive timely insights and fresh market research to help you wage the war for the small business market. To subscribe to this free weekly communiqué, please visit warrillow.com.

Appendix A
Partnership 2.0: The Next Generation of Partnership Strategies for Reaching the Small Business Market Successfully

Chapter 2 of this book advises you to supplement your media buy with a small business aggregator. Appendix A explains more specifically how to create a successful partnership by using the *customization principle,* a tool Warrillow & Co. developed to help Fortune 500 marketers create unique and relevant small business offers. The customization principle, which reveals how customization and synergy between product offer and communication channel are key to partnership success, was borne out of our analysis of hundreds of small business partnerships. To demonstrate how the customization principle works, I elucidate some of the partnerships covered in Chapter 2.

The Evolution of Partnership

The first generation of corporate partnerships targeting the small business market consisted primarily of discount offerings: a hotel would give certain credit card users 10 percent off or a courier company and an office supply store would offer discounts to each other's small business clientele. As the number of partnerships grew, discount offerings became generic and ultimately diluted: they no longer differentiated the partners from their competition. Armed with a small business credit card and an industry association membership, the average entrepreneur would have no trouble obtaining discounted courier service, hotel rooms, and office supplies.

Today, a second generation of small business partnerships is emerging. No longer reaping rewards with simple discount offers, small business marketers have begun to diversify their offerings, joining forces with other suppliers to create new products specifically designed to facilitate and streamline small business processes. The purpose of most new partnerships is to enhance a company's relevance to the small business market, therefore driving its small business sales.

The Customization Principle

Every partnership designed to reach the small business market has some unique elements—the players, the offer, and the reach in the small business market all vary from one alliance to the next. Yet each partnership can be distilled into two fundamental elements that can make or break its success:

- The product or service being offered
- The *contact channel,* the method used to communicate with the target market

These two elements can be customized to varying degrees. In the case of the product or service offering, the level of customization indicates how much the offer was modified to increase relevance to the small business market. Some products receive no customization: courier service from UPS works the same way no matter whom the company chooses as a partner. Others' products are highly customized, designed specifically with the small business market in mind.

Customization of the contact channel describes the extent to which a channel is high touch. A billboard is a noncustomized channel in which the target receives no individual contact, whereas one-to-one selling, a high-touch form of

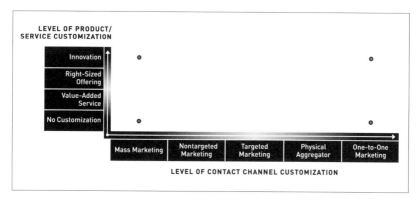

Figure A.1 Levels of Product/Service and Contact Customization

communication, is characterized by an extremely high level of customization.

As small business marketers move away from simple discount-based partnerships, the level of product and contact channel customization becomes increasingly important. Today's successful partnerships are generally characterized by a high level of product and/or contact channel customization. Outlined in Figure A.1 are the various levels of contact channel and product customization.

Levels of Contact Channel Customization

The contact channel is the method by which partners communicate with the target market. Generally speaking, as the contact channel grows more customized (high touch), the impact of the offer increases. Customization of contact channel falls into one of the following five categories, ranked here from least customized to most customized:

1. *Mass marketing:* The offer is communicated through nonpersonalized, static media channels such as print, radio, television, or billboards.

2. *Nontargeted marketing:* Outbound marketing initiatives communicate the offer. Examples of nontargeted marketing include inserts, flyers, brochures, and the company web site.

3. *Targeted marketing:* The offer is communicated through outbound, addressed marketing initiatives. Examples include e-mail, direct mail, or telemarketing offerings.

4. *Physical aggregator:* Physical aggregation occurs when one partner leverages the existing inbound foot traffic of the second partner to create a new, physical distribution channel.

5. *One-to-one sales:* A company's outbound sales force initiates face-to-face contact with the small business owner.

Levels of Product or Service Customization

The more a product is modified to enhance its relevance to small business, the higher the product's customization level. Typically, there are four levels of product or service customization. They are listed below from lowest to highest level of customization:

1. *No customization:* No changes are made to the existing product or service offering.

2. *Value-added service:* A partner adds a service from another company to add value to the overall offering.

3. *Right-sized offering:* A right-sized offering is a product or service currently offered to large businesses that has been scaled down to be more relevant to smaller businesses.

4. *Innovation:* Innovations are created when two or more partners combine strengths to offer a new product or service to the small business market. They are generally most successful when they leverage a key insight or an existing behavior of small businesses.

Success Depends on Moving Away from the Epicenter

First- and second-generation partnerships fall along a grid like the one shown in Figure A.2.

First-generation partnerships, as illustrated in the grid below, have little customization and are therefore clustered together in the grid's epicenter. As the number of first-generation partnerships grows, the offers become increasingly generic, losing much of their meaning in the small business market.

The farther a small business marketer moves along one or both axes, the more differentiation is created. Second-generation partnerships are characterized by more customization along the product and/or contact-channel axes, resulting in highly differentiated offerings (see Figure A.3).

As partnerships reaching the small business market become more and more customized, success becomes more dependent on moving away from the epicenter to develop differentiated and relevant small business offerings. As the following partnership examples demonstrate, strategic customization is key to creating a lift in small business sales by developing meaningful products and services to the small business market.

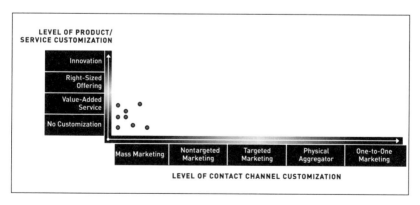

Figure A.2 First-Generation Partnerships

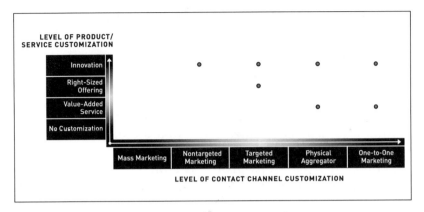

Figure A.3 Second-Generation Partnerships

The Customization Principle in Action

Using the customization principle, Warrillow & Co. here analyzes the strategies behind five successful small business partnerships. Each of these partners came together to reach the small business market, and all (except one, which has not yet been launched) have met or exceeded their own sales objectives.

The partnerships profiled in the following pages were formed for different reasons. But despite very different goals, each partner's fundamental strategy is the same: leverage at least one highly customized channel to differentiate itself against the diluted offerings of first-generation types of partnerships.

For each case study, a brief description of the partners' challenges and strategic plays is outlined below. Warrillow & Co. has added key partnership insights, including how the partners leveraged their customized channels, to each case study. The partnerships are arranged in order of product or service customization level.

No Customization

To be successful against the small business market, a partner-ship involving a noncustomized product needs a customized (i.e., high-touch) contact channel. Given enough relevance, a new contact channel can have a significant impact on sales. The Intuit partnership outlined below illustrates how an existing product can target a difficult-to-reach niche very effectively by leveraging existing behaviors to create a highly customized and relevant contact channel (see Figure A.4).

Business partner programs are relatively common in the small business market, but few make as much sense as Intuit's QuickBooks Affiliate Program (see Figure A.5). The program leverages both the synergy between product and channel and the relevance of the channel to the small business market.

Partnership: Intuit QuickBooks Affiliate Program

Partners' challenge

Accounting software is purchased early in the business life cycle, but the start-up market is difficult to reach because few direct mail lists effectively target this segment. Intuit, an accounting software provider, seeks new ways to reach the start-up market cost-effectively.

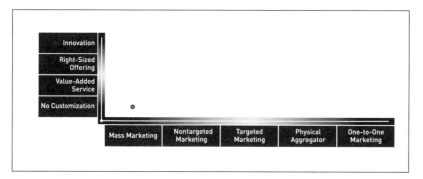

Figure A.4 No Customization

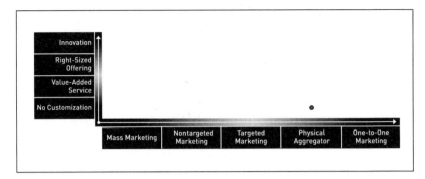

Figure A.5 Intuit QuickBooks Affiliate Program

Strategic play

Professionals offering business services, such as accountants and vertical market service providers, often have influence over the start-up market. Without a management committee or a board of directors to consult, start-up businesses go to trusted accountants and industry professionals for business insight and advice.

To leverage the small business/professional relationship, QuickBooks launched an Affiliate Program in fall 2000 whereby QuickBooks Financial Management software was sold via the websites of approved professionals. In exchange, affiliates receive incremental revenues by sales volume.

Contact channel

Accountants are contacted through the QuickBooks e-newsletter and direct mail. Information is also placed on the QuickBooks web site.

After accountants have registered, they sell QuickBooks Financial Management software to small businesses via their web sites.

Key partnership insights

Running a successful business-partner program is more difficult than it first appears. The key to a successful partnership with no product customization is choosing a highly customized (high-touch) and especially relevant channel. Intuit's success is based on the natural synergy between product and channel, and on the channel's built-in relevance to the small business market.

As primary small business influencers, accountants can be a potent contact channel. This is especially true in the case of accounting software: the opinion of a business owner's accountant is likely to matter less when it comes to choosing a courier or developing the company logo than it does when setting up financial processes.

No matter how relevant the product, however, Intuit needed cooperation from the channel to make this partnership a success. After surveying their client base and determining that 80 percent rely on their accountants for general business advice, Intuit courted the accounting market, creating the QuickBooks ProAdvisor Program. The program provides members with a free copy of QuickBooks Financial Management software, trial versions for clients, customizable reference materials, and more. At 25,000 members, the program is sizable enough to provide a strong base for the Intuit Affiliate program.

Value-Added Services

There are two types of value-added service partnerships (see Figure A.6).

- Product/product partnership: Each partner provides the other with a product or service to strengthen the overall offering.
- Product/channel partnership: One partner provides a product or service and leverages the distribution channel of the second partner to market the new offering.

A value-added service partnership is different from a business partner relationship. In the previous example, Intuit's business partners function as a distribution channel. How-

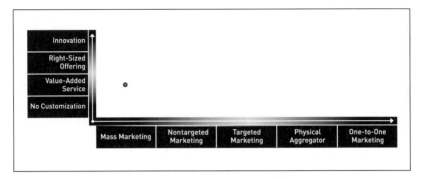

Figure A.6 Value-Added Services

ever, the availability of QuickBooks software is not a compelling enough reason for a small business owner to choose one accountant over another. By contrast, a value-added service should be compelling enough to act as a differentiator between the partner company and its competition.

Value-added service partnerships are often the domain of those businesses whose traditional offerings are considered commodities. Faced with an undifferentiated product and little price difference between competitors, office supply and courier companies engage in value-added partnerships to differentiate their product offerings from those of their competitors.

Unlike most partners offering a value-added service, Staples and ADP (Automatic Data Processing, Inc.) are using the highly customized physical aggregation strategy. Given the simplicity of the offering, face-to-face contact with customers is one of the partnership's key differentiators (see Figure A.7).

Collaboration: Staples and ADP

Collaborators' challenge
Office supply companies face a particularly difficult marketing challenge. Most of the items they sell are considered com-

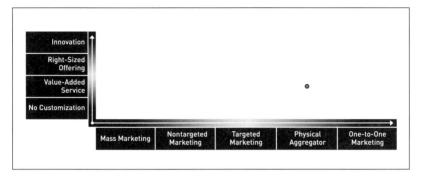

Figure A.7 Staples and ADP

modities and little price differentiation exists from one brand to the next. A few years ago, Staples developed an overall strategy to broaden the company's brand and add value to its existing product offerings.

Strategic play

After analyzing a variety of different services, Staples determined that adding payroll consultation to its existing offer made good sense. "Payroll processing is a universal need for small business; it's relevant to small business and we felt Staples would be a credible provider," said Mitch Gross, vice president of business services for Staples.

In April 2001 Staples and ADP partnered to launch an in-store payroll service for Staples' small business customers. ADP sales specialists staff ADP kiosks in nearly all of Staples' 1,000+ retail stores throughout the United States.

Contact channel

Staples is able to provide value-added services to the company's existing product offering, as well as use ADP's services as a differentiator in an otherwise unspecialized category.

ADP establishes a new face-to-face consultation channel reaching a large number of microbusinesses—the type of business most likely to do in-house payroll. A presence in

Staples' stores also offers ADP the opportunity to reach both small business owners and their administrators, the individuals often responsible for payroll.

Key partnership insights

The QuickBooks Affiliate Program outlined previously demonstrates how an uncustomized product can gain lift through a specialized, high-touch contact channel. The Staples/ADP partnership demonstrates how an uncustomized product can give new relevance to the contact channel. It may seem as though ADP is the big winner in this partnership, but Staples is gaining something equally as important but far less tangible: enhanced brand equity.

Says Mitch Gross: "The alliance gives us additional relevance to our small business customers—a very important segment of our client base. They now look at Staples in a different way . . . Payroll is critical to a company's operation, emotionally and financially. If small businesses rely on Staples as a provider of mission critical services, it can only help our brand."

Suppliers who offer relatively commodity-based products or services should look at partnership as a chance to boost relevance through association. Payroll companies, financial service providers, and certain industry suppliers have a pull in the small business market that few other suppliers can claim. Tying a less differentiated brand to that kind of mission critical service creates a positive association in the mind of small businesses.

Another key to this alliance's success is the use of the physical aggregation strategy. Many office supply companies offer value-added services through their web sites; however, a sizable number of their customers never visit the site. The ability to obtain a customized, face-to-face payroll consultation from an ADP representative should drive ADP sales higher than a website link alone and should drive Staples' brand equity even further than a stand-alone electronic connection.

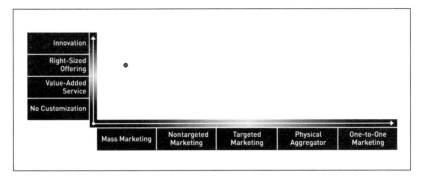

Figure A.8 Right-Sized Offering

Right-Sized Offering

Right-sized offerings are defined as those products or services traditionally offered to large businesses that have been scaled down, usually in scope, functionality, and price, to reflect more accurately the small business experience (see Figure A.8).

As relatively customized products, right-sized offerings are often unfamiliar to their small business audience. Many are also quite complex, and therefore a challenge to market effectively through noncustomized channels.

Partnership: Intuit, Citibank, and MasterCard

Partners' challenge

To boost their market share in the increasingly competitive small business credit card market, Citibank created a co-branded credit card with QuickBooks, the number-one small business software in the United States (see Figure A.9).

Strategic play

The alliance provided Citibank with access to one of the largest small business databases in the country as well as an

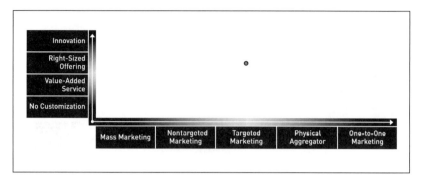

Figure A.9 Intuit, Citibank, and MasterCard

association with a well-respected small business brand: QuickBooks. The ability to download QuickBooks credit card data automatically and categorize it is a key selling feature of the product. This enables small businesses to track expenses, manage their cash flows, and track tax deductible expenses in a quick, easy way.

Beyond a recurring source of revenue, Intuit hopes to drive customer loyalty by providing small business owners with a new, value-added product. The card will also encourage software upgrades: Because the credit card can be used only with QuickBooks 2000 or 2001 software, small businesses using a previous version must upgrade to reap the card's benefits.

Contact channel
Citibank MasterCard is targeting the QuickBooks customer base through direct mail. Intuit will target its own base through e-mail, inserts in retail software boxes, and web marketing.

Key partnership insights
The popularity of this right-sized offering can be traced to functionality and a sizable built-in channel. "Most small business owners aren't accountants. But they have to reconcile the books," observes Sandy Kraft, Group Product Manager, Online Transactions, at Intuit. Entrepreneurs would rather

spend their time doing business than keeping track of it. Designers want to be designing; contractors and construction workers want to be on the job site; and service providers want to be out in front of their prospects selling. Any product that enables them to spend more time *doing* is likely to see great marketshare.

Despite a built-in potential audience of 2.8 million Quick-Books users, however, take rates were initially slow. While Kraft feels that the ability to identify and append business addresses to consumer direct mail efforts was a key challenge, leveraging Intuit's relationship with the accounting community would likely also have helped to increase initial sales.

The next two partnerships are based on a right-sized offering, using a physical aggregator as the contact channel. Both product and channel are relatively customized, creating a relevant offer communicated in a compelling way.

Partnership: American Express and Costco

The offering

American Express and Costco have created a co-branded credit card for the small business market (see Figure A.10). The card, the American Express Costco Corporate Card for Small Business, is free with the purchase of a $45 Costco

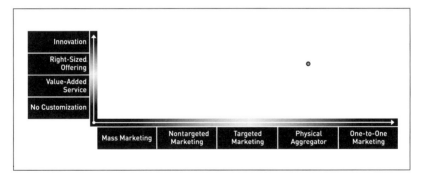

Figure A.10 American Express and Costco

Business Membership in the United States. In Canada, the card has a $59 membership fee but can be used in lieu of a membership card at all Costco outlets.

Strategic play

Costco sells products in volume, likely resulting in considerable average spend per visit. This allows American Express to increase retail spending on the card significantly without engaging in a prohibitive number of acceptance agreements.

In return, Costco members get a payment method that helps them separate business and personal expenditures. Value-driven Costco members also get access to American Express's Membership Rewards Program, which features discounts with partners such as Delta Airlines and FedEx.

Contact channel

Information tables and point-of-purchase pamphlets were available in Costco stores and the card was promoted both through direct mail and through membership renewal inserts. The card was also featured in *Costco Connection*, Costco's business publication with a United States circulation of 3.4 million.

Results

According to American Express's 2000 United States Annual Report, retail charge volume increased 48 percent on their cards from 1998 to 2000, compared to a 14 percent increase in travel charges during that same period. American Express attributes part of this growth to the success of the Costco partnership.

Key partnership insights

The American Express Costco Corporate Card for Small Business is not an overly customized product; however, it has appeal as a right-sized offer because it combines two sets of fees into one: the Costco membership and the American Express card annual fee. Value-driven small business customers now get the benefit of using both services for one smaller fee.

No matter how much small business owners love a deal, however, co-branded products work best if both brands, and both products, have direct relevance to the small business market. Both American Express and Costco are known for servicing the small business market and have a large, growing small business customer base. Because of the simplicity of the offering, this partnership may not have worked had the two brands originally enjoyed less reach in their target market.

Finally, few contact channels offer what Costco has given American Express: exclusivity. Being the only credit card accepted at Costco's 310 North American locations creates a powerful incentive for small business patrons to apply for the card.

Innovations

Innovations, new products or services created exclusively for the small business market, often necessitate a very customized (high-touch) contact channel (see Figure A.11). The product or service is new and therefore challenging to communicate through mass media or direct mail.

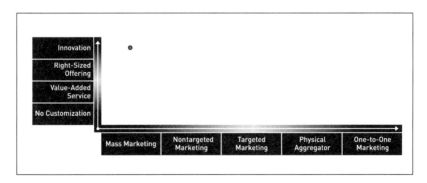

Figure A.11 Innovations

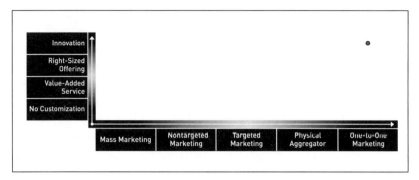

Figure A.12 Pfizer, Microsoft, and IBM

In the case of Pfizer, Microsoft, and IBM, a one-to-one sales approach will be used, a highly customized sales strategy.

Partnership: Pfizer, Microsoft, and IBM

The challenge

Approximately 70 percent of physicians in the United States work in small practices. Often understaffed and carrying full client loads, physicians indicate that the excessive paperwork associated with their profession is impacting patient care. Seventy percent of physicians surveyed for the 2000 Leadership Survey, conducted by the Health Information Management Systems Society, indicated that improving operating efficiencies was their primary workplace concern.

Strategic play

Record keeping in small physicians' offices is traditionally paper-based. Pfizer is collaborating with IBM and Microsoft to create a separate independent company, called Amicore, that will develop new software solutions designed to automate physician workflow and record keeping, including appointment scheduling, patient medical history recording, billing, coding, referral, and prescription writing (see Figure A.12). Medical information will be accessible in real time from a variety of devices including handheld units. To ensure that the cost is accessible to the target market, medical offices with fewer than twelve physicians, the software will be made available through the option of installing the Amicore Practice Suite as an integrated turnkey system in their office or adopting an Application Service Provider (ASP) model in which Amicore software and the customer's practice data reside at a secure IBM hosting facility accessible through the Internet.

The collaboration will enable Amicore to expand its product offering by leveraging the strengths of the three companies, while the collaborators also benefit. Pfizer is able to leverage its knowledge of the medical market and share in Amicore's success. Microsoft, which will gain a new distribution channel for its technology among small medical practices, will work with Amicore to enhance the product's technology architecture by leveraging its .Net platform, software, tools, and technology support. IBM's strategy is to collaborate with leading health care software vendors to approach health care customers. In line with that strategy, IBM will work closely with Amicore to aggregate the physician marketplace so that IBM can leverage its consulting, hardware, and services capabilities, especially the application hosting service.

Contact channel

Pfizer's 8,000-person in-field sales force is expected to leverage its existing relationships with physicians in small medical offices to build product awareness and market the new offering. Amicore will have its own stand-alone sales force to sell directly to the market and will accept leads from the Pfizer sales force. The new company sales representatives are expected to close the sale.

Key insights

Industry-specific innovations are generally the most customized, and as such the most relevant. The software is being developed for a specific industry and is designed to take care of industry-specific challenges. The benefits of the software are obvious and easy to sell. As such, one would expect the product to be an attractive offering to the health care marketplace. However, in order for physicians to use the software, they must alter several preexisting behaviors, which could prove detrimental to the product's ultimate success.

The handheld device with which doctors will record patient information is of particular concern. Since doctors are used to recording information manually, this wireless device may well prove cumbersome to the uninitiated doctor. Dr. Paul Ziter, who works in a small medical office, speculates that his underdeveloped typing skills would make real-time data entry very time-consuming. He suggests replacing the handheld device with voice recording technology that would enable him to capture information automatically using speech to text technology.

Another potential stumbling block is the use of the ASP model. Traditionally, ASPs have met with limited success in the small business market. Most entrepreneurs are fiercely protective of their businesses and dislike the idea of storing mission-critical or sensitive data, such as financial records or client information, off-site. In addition, a significant number of small businesses do not buy software at all, pirating from friends, families, or members of their professional networks instead.

However, small business owners, including physicians, may be more amenable to a vertical software application delivered via an ASP model. To begin with, vertical software is not as widely distributed, and therefore may be more difficult to borrow from personal connections. Tim Elwell, business development executive in IBM's health care unit, also points out that the ASP model will help streamline IT costs. "According to a PWC/Modern Physician study, a physician's office spends one to three percent of its operational budget on IT-related expenses. This means they can't afford large, sophisticated, stand-alone systems. So centralizing the technology using an ASP delivery model makes a lot of sense." Preliminary research conducted by Pfizer indicates that physicians are open to the ASP model if they see a cost benefit.

Selling a product that involves this much behavior alteration will no doubt be challenging. However, Pfizer's decision to leverage its existing sales force is a wise one. Because Pfizer is a vertical supplier, its sales force is likely to have significantly more clout with the medical community than an account representative from an office supply store or a value-added reseller. Leveraging the know-how and brand recognition of Pfizer, IBM, and Microsoft is expected to influence the purchase decision.

Conclusion

While the customization principle seems straightforward, enough permutations can be developed to help small business marketers with all of their marketing objectives. Staples used the principle to build brand equity. American Express used it to gain a powerful physical aggregator. Pfizer, IBM, and Microsoft are creating a market for a new and customized vertical software solution.

The key to successful partnerships is maximizing customization either along the product axis or along the contact channel axis. Although each situation is different, these general guidelines may be helpful:

- The more competitive the category, the more product customization is required
- The more complex the offering, the more contact-channel customization is required

As small business marketing becomes increasingly competitive, simple discount offers become decreasingly sufficient to change behavior. Marketers need to become more and more relevant in order to be successful at capturing their targets.

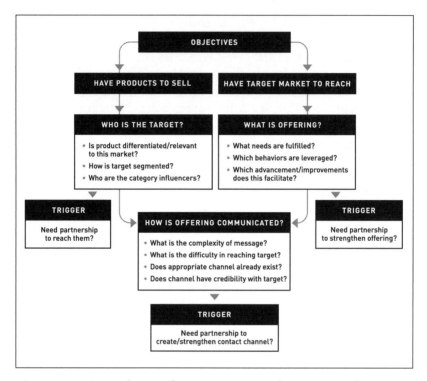

Figure A.13 High-Level Trigger Points for Partnership

The Partnership Decision Tree

Deciding what level of product and contact channel customization is needed to create successful partnerships is not easy. The following is a high-level overview of the questions that marketers should consider as triggers to partnership (see Figure A.13).

Appendix B
Small Business Marketing Campaigns That Resonate

As is explained in Chapter 3 of this book, no hard and fast rules exist for creating a small business marketing campaign. However, I do realize that small business marketers would like to see some recent examples of campaigns that captured the attention of entrepreneurs. For this reason I include this appendix, which features 10 interesting small business marketing campaigns from the last few years.

Each campaign was selected because of a unique insight or tactic. These are by no means the only successful marketing campaigns targeting small business (in fact, some of the companies highlighted were significantly impacted in the so-called tech wreck of the past two years), but they are full of lessons useful to marketers.

In order to give you an idea of each of these small business marketers' unique challenges and creative approaches, I provide a case study of each campaign that includes background, objectives, strategy, creative approach, and results. At the end of each case study, I explain why I find the campaign is interesting and which important insights make it worth a mention in this book.

Marketer: FMC Corporation, Agricultural Products Division

Campaign
Capture Insecticide Brand Awareness Campaign (see Figure B.1)

If you think you have nothing to learn from a campaign for insecticide, think again. FMC's Capture Insecticide campaign demonstrates the power of truly understanding the motivations of your vertical market. In addition, it underscores the benefits of working with your distribution network to more effectively reach small business.

Agency
The Martin Agency

Background
In 2000, FMC introduced Capture insecticide into the highly competitive midwestern corn-growers' market. Because a number of well-established companies were already leaders in this field, FMC and the Martin Agency knew that they would need a spectacular campaign to be successful. They also had another challenge in converting their audience; studies had shown them that farmers were typically skeptical of trying new things.

Primary target
This campaign was targeted at a very specific vertical market within the small business sector—farmers in the midwestern United States with at least 250 acres of corn planted.

Secondary target
Agricultural chemical dealers who sold FMC products.

Figure B.1 Capture Insecticide
Source: Courtesy of FMC Corporation

Objectives
- To build brand awareness in a new agricultural segment
- To ensure that agricultural chemical dealers in the region were aware and informed of the product and its usage

Strategy
"Farmers fight a constant battle in their fields. The strategy was to recognize their war in a way that rallies them to keep fighting," says Sydney Giffen Norton of the Martin Agency. "We wanted Capture insecticide to stand for hope and empowerment and to reinforce their survivalist instinct."

Through creative graphics, FMC wanted to give farmers the message that Capture could protect them from Mother Nature and preserve the profitability of their farms. The strategy, says Giffen Norton, was to come on strong "in a smart way." Recognizing that farmers often feel at the mercy of the environment, Capture was to symbolize giving them back some control.

Simultaneously, they wanted to inform the dealers about the product in order to to ensure that when farmers went into the store asking about Capture, they got it.

Creative approach

Through mass marketing, a consistent message was established across all channels focusing on the battle that farmers wage against pests (see Figure B.2). The tag line was "Because we don't have to!" One television execution featured these lines:

> Why don't we give our corn to the insects?
> Hey, why don't we give our kites to the trees?
> Why don't we give our libraries to the loud?
> Why don't we just give our picnics to the ants?
> Why don't we give our corn to the insects?
> *Because we don't have to.*
> Capture Insecticide. Any pest. Every time.

Very graphic visuals in the various executions included a child holding an ice cream covered in flies, kites caught in trees, a young woman swimming in a pool filled with algae, and picnickers covered in ants. The images were particularly striking because their somewhat shocking content was juxtaposed against soft music and slow camera movement. The print campaign was simple, yet effective. It featured a cornfield with military troops on guard where the roots would be.

The dealer marketing was coupled with information about other FMC products. The first contact was a big box that included a store display, product brochures, and a flip book showing military men beating up rootworms. Following this contact was a specific mailing which focused exclusively

Figure B.2 Capture Insecticide
Source: Courtesy of FMC Corporation

on Capture (subsequent mailings featured the other FMC products).

Contact method

FMC and the Martin Agency used an integrated media plan, targeting farmers with television, radio, and print. Public relations and trade show efforts also reinforced the message.

The TV and radio spots ran in key agricultural markets

throughout the midwest, including a heavy TV schedule on AgDay, a syndicated daily agricultural news program. The print ads appeared in *Farm Journal,* the most widely recognized agricultural trade journal.

Chemical dealers were targeted with a direct mail component.

Cost of campaign

The overall budget, including the dealer marketing and the media spending, was approximately $1.6 million.

Results

The product was launched a mere six months from press time; however, by the end of the first quarter, FMC was already 55 percent of the way to meeting its aggressive 2001 goals.

An advertising tracking study is currently in field; it will measure advertising awareness and main message recall.

Follow-up

While all the results are not yet in, the initial success has lead FMC to continue with the strategy for the rest of 2001. In addition, the campaign was specifically designed so that it would be transferable to other crops (although some of the creative will have to be changed) and other markets. It will, therefore, be introduced over time.

Why it works

This campaign is an excellent example of targeting a vertical market in the small business arena. The media buy was extremely well targeted to reach this market. Industry verticals, when bought correctly, are a very efficient and effective way to reach the small business owner. For instance, 98 percent of the 575,000 subscribers to Farm Journal are small business owners.[1]

1. Warrillow & Co., "Media Habits of the SmallBusiness Owner," *Warrillow Report* 01, no. 01.

The use of traditional media rather than e-mail or web-based advertising reflects FMC's understanding of its market. A 1999 E-Market Dynamics study showed that only 33 percent of small businesses in agriculture and mining used e-mail, as compared to 64 percent of all small businesses in the United States.[2]

The message is communicated very effectively and is completely on-target. The humor reinforces the positioning rather than detracts from it. They have shown good insight into the market by recognizing that farmers sometimes feel powerless over their environment; they position Capture as not only a pesticide, but also a method of gaining and maintaining control over the adverse factors that affect their livelihood.

The Capture campaign also illustrates the importance of the sales channel in targeting the small business market. A significant number of small business technology purchases are made through VARs, most travel is booked through a travel agent, and, in this case, getting cooperation from agricultural chemical dealers was crucial for success.

Creatively, we loved the contrast between the strong, sometimes disturbing imagery and the slow movement and comforting music. The images were very bold and effective, really giving the brand a personality.

Even if you don't market insecticide, farmers are a market to consider in your marketing efforts. In the year 2000, there were 2,172,080 farms in the United States, up from 1,911,859 in 1997 (an increase of 13 percent). In 1999, net farm income in the United States totalled $43.4 billion. In addition, financial services marketers may be interested to know that United States farms held a total $176.4 billion in outstanding debt at the end of 1999.[3]

---

2. E-Market Dynamics, *Exploring U.S. Small Business Vertical Markets*, 1999.
3. U.S. Department of Agriculture.

Marketer: RBC Royal Bank of Canada

Campaign
Appreciation Phase IV (see Figure B.3)

The fabulous response rates to this direct mail campaign speak for themselves. Simple creative with a nonmarketing feel acted as an incredibly effective call to action for the small business market. We also liked the fact that RBC Royal Bank recognizes that client data is crucial to an effective small business marketing strategy.

Agency
Cossette Communications Group

Background
Like many small business marketers, RBC Royal Bank of Canada recognized that the quality of its data was the key to its success in future marketing efforts; thus, in 1998 the RBC Royal Bank initiated a comprehensive cleanup of their business-to-business database, using aggressive customer con-

Figure B.3 RBC Royal Bank of Canada
Source: Courtesy of Royal Bank of Canada

tact strategies like telemarketing. Over the following 12 months, they successfully contacted approximately 40 percent of the customer base, updating customer profile information and contact preferences.

This left 60 percent of the customers on the database with their information unverified. RBC Royal Bank's base rule is that no customer should be included in any marketing activities until they have been *appreciated* (i.e., have had their contact information and preferences verified). Therefore, the bank wanted to find a quick and cost-effective method of making this contact.

Target

The target audience was business-banking customers who had not been successfully contacted via the previous customer appreciation telemarketing efforts. Of particular interest were customers with a positive revenue value and moderate-to-low credit risk. A sample of 25,000 was randomly selected from their database.

Objectives

- To verify and update contact information and identify the contact preferences of the RBC Royal Bank business-banking customer base, thus allowing these customers to be targeted with the bank's revenue-generating and loyalty CRM initiatives
- To provide cost-effective alternative contact methods while cleansing the balance of the nonappreciated Business Banking customer base
- To obtain updated customer information from 20 percent of the target audience in this test

Strategy

The bank decided to test the effectiveness and compare the cost per response of a direct mail approach against previous efforts using outbound telemarketing and data appending (rented lists were matched to get phone numbers). This was a learning initiative that was to be continued if successful.

The strategy was to create a piece that would elicit response by appearing as an official bank request rather than a marketing initiative.

Creative approach

The self-mailer was designed to look similar to a tax receipt or official bank document. In keeping with the tax form concept, no sales or marketing messages and no offers were included in the piece. The piece was designed to be monochromatic, and the copy focused entirely on the need to update contact information.

The piece read: "At RBC Royal Bank, we are currently updating our records so that we can continue to provide our Business Banking customers with the highest possible level of service. Please take a few minutes to verify the information below and add any missing information. As well, please answer a short list of questions. Thank you for your time." It went on to ask basic contact details along with primary decision maker's name and relationship to the business, language preference, and preferred communication method (telephone, mail, e-mail, fax).

Contact method

The bank used a direct mail self-mailer. Response was postage paid, or could be done by fax or through the call center.

Cost of campaign

The test mailing cost under $17,000; this represented a unit cost of less than $0.70 per piece.

Results

The test mailing generated a 35.5 percent response rate, exceeding the original objective by over 77 percent. This resulted in a cost per response of only $1.80. Although the contact ratio was slightly higher using telemarketing, that method's cost per contact was $8.00, making the mailer a much more attractive option.

Follow-up

The results of this mailing exceeded all of RBC Royal Bank's expectations. Because this test campaign was so successful, it has not only replaced the previous control contact strategy for first point of contact, but is also being used to update and expand continuously the customer information files of the entire base.

Why it works

This campaign illustrates that you do not have to be flashy or advertise during the Super Bowl to get results. The incredible response rate to such a low-cost initiative is testament to the effectiveness of the strategy. While a no-cost call to action (i.e. respondents do not have to make a purchase) typically generates higher responses, this campaign is still in a class of its own.

This campaign also illustrates that small businesses will provide information if they see a reason. Crucial to gathering preference information, however, is the ability to utilize the responses. We caution all marketers to gather information from their clients *only* if it will be used to improve their marketing strategies and client service. RBC Royal Bank tells us that after they capture the customer's indicated preference, (barring any legal restrictions such as price changes or official notifications), they always communicate with the client using that channel. Almost all of their marketing materials are launched in e-mail, mail, and telephone to cover all available preferences.

Because the piece appeared to be an official bank request, it likely generated response across all small business groups— Mountain Climbers, Freedom Fighters, and Craftspeople. We question how well this strategy would work for marketers in other industries, however. Banks have a different relationship and a stronger leverage with small business owners from office-supply providers or online portals.

This strategy also shows two additional insights into the market. Small business owners deal with a lot of official forms and receipts, and are more likely to pay attention to them. The inclusion of a fax option for response is also right on target; even very small businesses have a fax machine.

The campaign also illustrates how vital it is to maintain your customer database. Inaccurate data leads to wasted dollars through inappropriate targeting and undeliverable messages. Using poor information will erode the trust you are working so hard to build with small business. The increased revenue from improved targeting will easily offset reasonable investments in clean data.

Marketer: AllBusiness

Campaign
Brand Launch (see Figures B.4 and B.5)

This mass media branding campaign was clearly targeted at the Mountain Climber segment of small business. We were impressed by AllBusiness's ability to tap into the emotional state of this group and to truly convey a personality for their brand. The ads were engaging and humorous without being condescending.

Agency
Butler, Shine and Stern

Background
AllBusiness is one of many small business portals that have launched in the past couple of years. Given the intense competition in this marketplace, it was critical that this campaign, their brand launch, served to differentiate them from other portals. They did considerable research to determine the characteristics of their target audience and to develop a brand that would resonate.

Target
Although AllBusiness serves the broader small business market (companies with 100 or fewer employees), the campaign focused on the group they call Evangelists. The Evangelist segment is comprised of business owners, entrepreneurs, and intrapreneurs whose inspiration and energy drive small busi-

Figure B.4 AllBusiness

Source: Courtesy of AllBusiness.com

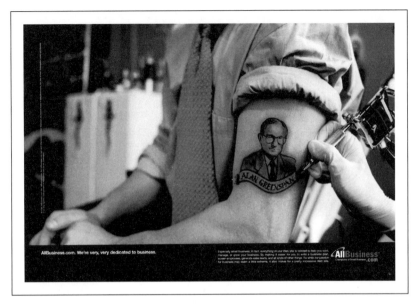

Figure B.5 AllBusiness
Source: Courtesy of AllBusiness.com

nesses forward. According to their research, this segment is also more active than any other in finding business solutions on the Internet.

Objectives

- To position AllBusiness as the leading web resource for entrepreneurs at all stages of their business growth
- To differentiate the brand with the positioning that AllBusiness was as passionate about business as the entrepreneurs whom they targeted

Strategy

In the company's research, the common denominator among Evangelists was a passion for their businesses and a strong desire to succeed. The strategy was to tap into the passion of the target audience through a positioning as *absurdly dedicated to business*. The company felt this positioning differentiated its image from that of the competitors in the same market, who sought a problem-solving image. AllBusiness wanted to convey the personality of the brand and reach out to the target audience on a human level.

Creative approach

Playing on the *absurdly dedicated to business* theme, the print and outdoor components featured images of a bride in her wedding dress sitting at her computer, someone receiving a tattoo of Alan Greenspan and a child wearing a t-shirt bearing the words "My daddy went to the Detroit Tax Planning Conference and all I got was this lousy t-shirt."

We asked David Jones, director of brand marketing and customer experience, why the marketers felt that Alan Greenspan was appropriate for the target market. "He stands for the net economy," enthused Jones. "He is a demigod of business." He went on to say that the selection was fortunate because Greenspan was just rising in popularity; consequently, the ads coincided with significant Greenspan coverage in the popular press.

The television spots used humor to reinforce the tagline "We are very, very dedicated to business." The first spot, entitled "Clinic," features a man at a sperm bank who furtively rejects racier reading material in favor of *Business Age* magazine "for inspiration." The graphic "Intensive Care" (see Figure B.6) spot shows a man disconnecting himself from IV tubes and oxygen to drag himself across the room to tune into a television program called "Business Hour." Finally, "Pet Shop" features a man looking at an adorable puppy sitting in the window of a pet shop. He taps on the window to indicate his interest and the store assistant lifts the dog for him to see. He, of course, is only interested in the newspaper's business section on top of which the puppy was sitting.

Contact method

AllBusiness used targeted print publications (such as *Inc.,* *Business 2.0,* and *Entrepreneur*) as the sole national media vehicle. Local markets were targeted based on their composition of small business and online penetration; broadcast was

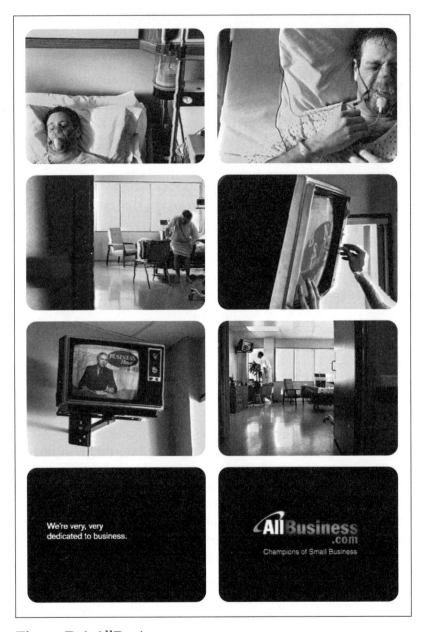

Figure B.6 AllBusiness

Source: Courtesy of AllBusiness.com

used primarily in New York, San Francisco and LA, where the company's marketers estimated they could reach 25 percent of their entire audience. Media used in local markets included TV spots, local business journals, and targeted magazines.

Television was the lead element (well over 50 percent of the budget) based on its ability to convey the brand image effectively. Early morning, late news, and late fringe were the times selected based on research and intuition. The marketers knew their target audience lived and breathed their businesses. "We decided there was little rationale for buying expensive primetime which the target has little affinity for in the first place . . . and even less time for in their day-to-day schedules," said David Jones.

Online banner ads reinforced the message; these ads carried such slogans as "Sex or work? | Tough call" and "Please don't squeeze the Charmin | It ruins inventory and kills profit margins." These banner ads were run primarily on distribution partner sites such as www.NBCi.com, www.CNBC.com, and www.about.com.

Cost of campaign
Approximately $8 million

Results:
Aided awareness jumped from under three percent to nearly seven percent in six months.

AllBusiness estimates that seventy-five percent of traffic during this period came from the offline advertising; this was evidenced by individuals typing AllBusiness.com into their browsers. Spikes on the company's tracking charts show direct correlation between advertising and page views.

According to analysis compiled by AllBusiness (based on figures from Media Matrix), their unique visit/advertising spend ratio was far better than that of their primary competitors. They estimated a 1:1 ratio compared to 1:2 for Onvia and 1:8 for Office.com.

One additional benefit that AllBusiness has discovered is that the campaign speaks to the company's employees too;

employees believe that the taglines are not simply words. They are engaged by and enthusiastic about the message, and they convey the attitude externally. To prove it, they wear t-shirts bearing slogans from the campaign such as "Thank God it's Monday" and sport Greenspan tattoos (temporary, we presume).

Follow-up

The campaign strategy is set to continue as AllBusiness integrates with BigVine over the next few months.

Why it works

We love this campaign because it speaks so clearly to the Mountain Climber Segment. The ads were targeted directly at the segment of small business owners absurdly dedicated to their businesses. We at Warrillow have seen too many marketers dilute their psychographic targeting, and thus their marketing effectiveness, to be more inclusive. It is more important to be something to someone than to be nothing to everyone.

Reaching out to the Mountain Climber segment is an excellent strategy; they lead and seed the market. Although they represent only 10 percent of small business owners, they are early adopters and have considerable influence over others.

AllBusiness used humor not to poke fun at small business owners, but rather to create an image for the brand. This was intelligent humor that resonates with the target segment. Although the product or service offerings differentiating All-Business from its competitors may not have been completely clear, the target won't quickly forget the AllBusiness name and its passion.

They also made some good media buys that reflect their target; they avoided prime time (when Mountain Climbers are still working) and selected appropriate local markets. Rather than focusing exclusively on the small business media, marketers trying to reach Mountain Climbers should consider the daily business press such as the Wall Street Journal. Only 6.6 percent of entrepreneurs we polled said they regularly read a small business magazine.[4]

Marketer: Office.com

Campaign
"Win a Million Dollar Bonus" Sweepstakes (see Figure B.7)

While Winstar, Office.com's parent company, is feeling the effects of the tech wreck, Office.com remains operational and I include this campaign in the marketing section because it so eloquently illustrates the power of word of mouth in the small business marketplace. Capitalizing on the small business owner's reliance on referrals, Office.com built its subscriber base and raised awareness of its service through viral marketing. We at Warrillow & Co. also like the fact that they were talking to individuals at small businesses, not to the business itself.

Agency
Radical Communication

Background:
Competing among dozens of sites targeting small- and medium-sized businesses, Office.com (www.Office.com) was challenged to attract new visitors and provide them with reasons to return regularly. Acquisition and retention were critical to success in a market in which so many sites were vying for the same small business audience.

Through focus group research, Office.com learned a valuable lesson on segmentation—the small business market is not homogeneous; the needs of each industry vertical are distinct. However, a lack of information about prospects and a desire to keep costs low meant the development of only one promotion. The challenge was to develop a marketing mes-

---

4. Warrillow & Co., "Media Habits of the Small Business Owner," *Warrillow Report* 01, no. 01.

sage that would effectively communicate the value proposition of Office.com to a diverse audience of people.

Target

The real target was people who work at small businesses, not necessarily those who own or run them. They rented external e-mail lists of known small businesses. In addition, all current Office.com registrants received the e-mail—although the eventual target was the friends and influencers that they referred. In total, 400,000 e-mails were initially sent—the bulk of which were from external e-mail lists.

Objectives

- To introduce the Office.com brand and service to a broader audience
- To attract new users through site registrations (giving Office.com permission to contact respondents on a regular, long-term basis)

Strategy

The strategy was to capture the attention of all potential Office.com users with a single message and a grand prize with universal appeal—cash. The plan was to use e-mail viral marketing (the refer-a-friend principle) to deliver the message to a much larger audience; the theory was that people were more willing to read and respond to e-mail that they had received from a friend.

A key component of the strategy was that the message and prize were designed to appeal to individuals—the money was to be for personal use, not products for one's business.

Creative approach

A streaming video e-mail was sent to e-mail lists and current subscribers. It played one of three Office.com television commercials; in addition, it contained a call to action to play the Office.com "Million Dollar Bonus Game & Sweepstakes" by linking back to the Office.com site. The e-mail message contained a field for users to forward it to a friend. By doing so,

Radical Communications could continue to track the results and path of responses to the e-mail from their friend referrals.

The viral marketing component continued when users went to Office.com and played the sweepstakes; here they were offered a chance to earn entries to win a Mercedes-Benz by forwarding this same e-mail to their friends. The "tell-a-friend" sweepstakes page enabled users to send the e-mail to up to four friends daily. Consequently, these referrals could come back and play the game and refer their friends—and so on, until the game ended.

The streaming video in the e-mail was the heart of the campaign and, according to Office.com, was the reason for its success. It provided a novelty that many users wanted to share with their friends.

Cliff Freeman and Partners developed the ads that were used for Office.com's brand launch. The television campaign featured 3 spots with the same copy: "Some people are always thinking, obsessed with finding better answers and solutions. For them, there is Office.com." They positioned Office.com as "The Internet workplace with the tools and resources businesspeople need most." Each execution features an individual getting a bright idea (as indicated by a bell going off) in a most unlikely place—then turning to Office.com in order to follow through on it.

The first ad features a man interrupting his jog to work out a complex formula in the dirt on the back of a cube van. Once done, he returns to the office and goes to Financial Pricing Models at Office.com to finish his thoughts. The second execution (Figure B.7) features a woman at a diner designing a dress on the table—using ketchup and mustard—with Office.com's Textile Design page on the laptop beside her. The final ad, "Doctor's Office," shows a man redesigning his office on the sterile bed covering while waiting for the doctor and racing out in his hospital gown to borrow the receptionist's computer for his Office.com visit.

The marketing messages in the e-mail and sweepstakes promotion were consistent with those in the general advertising campaign and therefore served to reinforce it.

Figure B.7 Office.com

Contact method
E-mail

Cost of campaign
While Office.com didn't provide us with the cost, we do know that no one actually won the million dollars (they had to guess a sequence of correct numbers to win). They did give away a 2000 Mercedes convertible to a retired autoworker.

Results
The e-mail itself generated considerable interest:

- Click-through rate: 72 percent of people who opened the e-mail clicked through to Office.com
- Conversion rate: 14 percent (some were already registered users)

- Cost per lead: Cost per new acquired member was $1.72
- Office.com exceeded its goal of doubling new users by 280 percent

The viral marketing component was also extremely effective. Of the people who played the sweepstakes, each person sent the e-mail to an average of 2 friends. Of these, 20 percent were opened, and 72 percent of the people who opened the e-mail came back to Office.com and played the sweepstakes. These friend referrals accounted for 39 percent of all the people who played the sweepstakes.

Why it works

The tactics were innovative and the creative approach was great. The ads speak well to small business and illustrate some uses of Office.com. Consistency with the branding campaign reinforces the effectiveness of both campaigns.

We particularly like the recognition that, while Office.com is marketing small business services, they are truly targeting consumers—people who work at small businesses. The use of the Office.com site is really not a company buying decision, but rather a personal one. As a result, a consumer prize resonates well here.

Small business owners rely heavily on referrals from their network of trusted individuals. As a result, member-get-member approaches work well for this market.

However, a contest may attract some people to register who have no intention of becoming users. Getting permission to contact the entire group and the ability to track their behavior probably makes up for this. In fact, although they would not provide the unsubscribe rate of sweepstakes players (an indication of those who came only for the contest), they do claim that it is no different from the industry average.

Caution should be used in applying this approach to other industries. Because Office.com's offering is an online one, one would presume a higher instance of Internet use than average. Although a majority of small businesses are online, many are on a dial-up account; consequently, e-mails that take considerable time to download may be annoying to your market. Office.com did tell us that a text version of the e-mail, containing a link to the web rather than video, was sent to those without the ability to read HTML. This approach may be preferable for some marketers.

Office.com is a trademark of Winstar Communications, Inc. and is used by permission.

Marketer: The Loyalty Group – AIR MILES for Business

Campaign
Spring 2000 Farmers Campaign (see Figures B.8 and B.9)

No other campaign we saw this year came close to The Loyalty Group's one-to-one targeting of farmers. Personalization is the logical next step for small business marketers—The Loyalty Group is ahead of its time.

Agency
Ogilvy Worldwide

Background
The AIR MILES® Reward Program is Canada's most successful consumer loyalty program, with over 50 percent of the population enrolled. In 1995, AIR MILES formed a Farmers' Coalition featuring agricultural-based sponsors such as United Grain Growers (UGG), John Deere Credit, Agline, Shell, and Goodyear. This group is now a critical segment of the AIR MILES For Business Program™, which targets the small business marketplace.

Primary target
50,000 farm collectors in western Canada who had made a purchase from one or more of the AIR MILES farm sponsors

Figure B.8 AIR MILES for Business
Source: Courtesy of The Loyalty Group

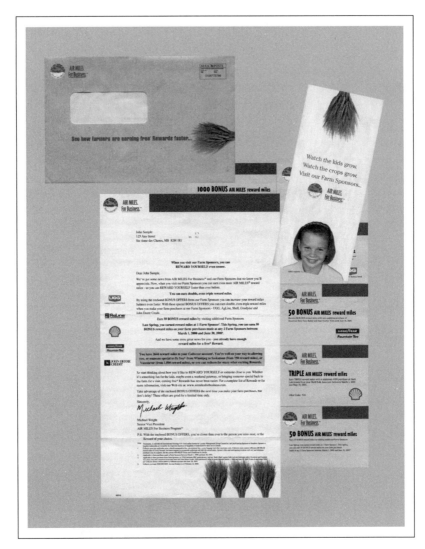

Figure B.9 AIR MILES for Business

Source: Courtesy of The Loyalty Group

in the previous 14 months. Database work was done to help sponsors understand and select the target market.

Secondary target

Any western Canadian farmer

Objectives

- To increase collector activity at farm sponsors
- To encourage use of multiple farm sponsors
- To continue to build awareness of the **AIR MILES** For Business Farm Coalition.

Strategy

The plan was to create a specialized **AIR MILES** For Business campaign targeted at the farming marketplace—recognizing their unique business needs with specialized copy and relevant offers. The strategy included leveraging the rich data in the collector database to personalize the creative execution to each collector.

Creative approach

The campaign consisted of a brochure and a letter and coupon sheet personalized based on the collector's past behavior at each of the farm sponsors. The key message was "Visit our farm sponsors and reward yourself or someone close to you." Two creative executions were tested in focus groups with farm collectors during development and the leading creative execution was introduced in the campaign.

The execution is an excellent example of one-to-one marketing to a small business audience:

- There were 72 different combinations of letter copy and 2,952 coupon sheet combinations completely driven by past behavior at **AIR MILES** farm sponsors.
- Not only did past behavior dictate which coupons someone received, but the offers from any one sponsor typically varied depending on whether it was an acquisition or retention offer to that particular cus-

tomer. Many sponsors also tested the effectiveness of different offers (i.e., different award levels) within this campaign.

- The letter included a variable reward message based on the collector's account balance and available rewards in his or her geographic region.
- It also incorporated a variable activation offer. It was linked to one coupon and provided an incentive for the collector to go to one sponsor more than they had the previous spring. This was personalized, telling the collector how many farm sponsors they used the year before.

The print campaign used the theme "Watch the kids grow. Watch the crops grow. Watch your AIR MILES reward miles grow. *Reward Yourself.*"

Contact method
This campaign was integrated, consisting of print and personalized direct mail.

The print advertising consisted of full-color ads in six Farm Business Communication Publications, as well as free brochures in retail locations of farm sponsors.

The direct mail included an outer envelope, personalized letter, lasered coupon, and a brochure.

Results
Twelve percent of those targeted used at least one of the offers in the mailing. In addition, six percent responded to the incentive of visiting one or more additional farm sponsors during the four-month promotional period.

Follow-up
This was actually the sixth AIR MILES Farmers Coalition collector mailing. The fact that it has become an annual program is testament to its effectiveness. In fact, in 2001, this Farm Coalition Program has been expanded to Atlantic Canada and Ontario.

AIR MILES For Business cites the success of this western campaign as a critical selling feature in attracting new sponsors to the program in these other regions.

These results and learnings have enhanced and benefited the other coalitions within the AIR MILES For Business Program.

Why it works

This campaign is a wonderful example of how data can be leveraged to make communications truly one-to-one. The AIR MILES database is the envy of many in direct marketing for the richness of the information it contains. The personalization in this campaign made entrepreneurs feel understood because the offers were targeted directly to them.

"It is almost unfair to compare them to other marketers," says Ellen Reid Smith, founder of Reid Smith and Associates and author of *eLoyalty.* "Most people think the value of loyalty programs is in the points and rewards. Fifty percent of the value is in the data collected. The value is in getting people to raise their hands and want to be tracked. The knowledge base is a gold mine."

The "Collect for Business. Travel for Pleasure" slogan works for the small business market. In our study on loyalty programs, we learned that 80 percent of small business owners surveyed use at least some of the points collected from loyalty programs (used for business) on themselves personally. Of those, 45 percent say that they spend the majority of their points earned on themselves personally.[5]

They took this strategy even further for this vertical market with the comment about "bringing someone special back to the farm for a visit"; they knew that many farming families have loved ones who have gone away to school or work and that this approach would appeal to such families.

Although the AIR MILES program is not available in the United States, this campaign illustrates the value of partner-

5. Warrillow Report, "The Impact of Loyalty Programs on the Buying Behaviors of Small Business Owners," *The Warrillow Report* 04, no. 01.

ing with others to reach the small business market. Effective partnering means that both partners can reach a wider audience and reach a better understanding of their prospects.

Marketer: VanCity Credit Union

Campaign
Small Loan Program (see Figures B.10 and B.11)

Financial institutions and small business often have a strained relationship. This campaign by the VanCity Credit Union used a clear customer-centered message to reach this market. Getting cooperation from the sales force also meant that the advertising message was carried through to the customer experience—a component too often missing from campaigns.

Agency
Grey World Wide: Vancouver

Background
In discussions with small business owners about their banking needs, financing was a recurring theme. However, VanCity had not been able to capitalize on this need because branch employees were reluctant to offer loans to small businesses because of the complexity and time involved in completing an application.

Thus, VanCity decided to revise the lending process to make it simpler for the branch to meet the needs of small business. A new one-page application form (Figure B.10) was developed to save staff time and make the process easier. In the words of one branch manager, "under the previous system, it typically took a lender two and one-half to five hours to complete the paperwork . . . [in the new system] staff took an average of twenty minutes to fill out an application." In addition, VanCity implemented an automated system from Fair

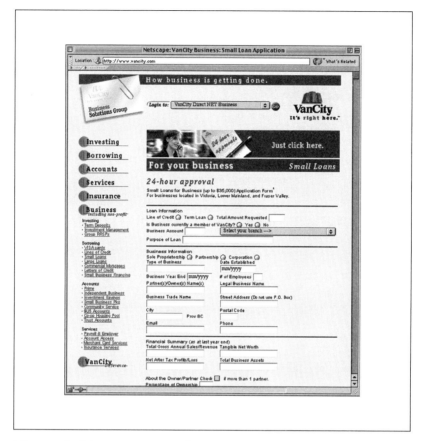

Figure B.10 VanCity Credit Union
Source: Courtesy of VanCity

Issac to ensure credit approval could be given within a day—through instant approval where appropriate and links to the back office for manual adjudication.

Recognizing that the small business owner's time is valuable, VanCity set out to capitalize on the new system and make this improvement a point of competitive differentiation in the small business market.

VanCity is Canada's largest credit union, with $6.4 billion in assets, 262,000 members, and 39 branches throughout British Columbia.

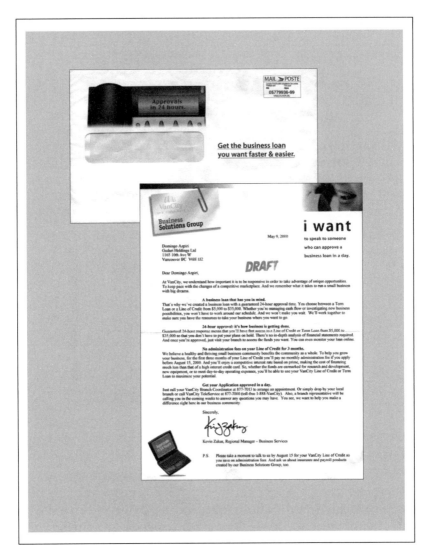

Figure B.11 VanCity Credit Union

Source: Courtesy of VanCity

Primary target

A sample of approximately 7,000 customers with no current lending products was selected. Analysis was done on the current loan portfolio to identify characteristics of customers with high propensity for lending and high likelihood of paying back their loans.

Secondary target

Small businesses not currently using VanCity

Objectives

- To sell term loans and lines of credit valued at between Can$5,000 and Can$35,000 (the target was 1–2 percent growth in new loans sold)
- To support the launch of a new small business loan system and new sales processes
- To increase public awareness of VanCity as a business solutions provider because VanCity has not traditionally been well known for small business services.

Strategy

According to Margot Davis, marketing manager for business at VanCity, the real hook was the "approvals within 24 hours" promise to clients. VanCity recognized that small businesses not only want a fast decision, but they also need to know when they will have an answer. The strategy was to communicate this promise through an integrated campaign centered on a direct-mail piece. The direct mail was supported by telephone follow-up and advertising.

A pilot program was introduced in 10 branches to test the lending system and sales training. During this period, hype was created in the other branches through e-mail testimonials and a special edition newsletter detailing the pilot's success. Expansion to the remaining 29 branches followed.

Also, for the first time in VanCity's business marketing group, sales incentives and a sales contest were staged.

Creative approach

The creative focused on the speed of approval (24-hour guarantee) and ease of application for small business loans under Can$35,000. The slogan was "I *want* someone who can approve a business loan in a day."

The direct-mail envelope featured a display phone with the copy "Get the business loan you want faster and easier." The letter focused on the 24-hour approval and a time-limited offer of no administrative fees.

Contact method

The campaign included the following elements:

- Direct mail (staggered every two weeks)
- Telephone follow-up
- Local newspaper advertisement (community and business papers)
- Radio (during introductory period only)
- Branch posters
- A fact sheet (collateral material for branch sales staff)
- Web site components (banner, online application, product detail)

Cost of campaign

Approximately $30,000

Results

The campaign garnered a 9 percent net response rate (completed sales) after approvals (approval rates varied between 60 and 85 percent). This response rate was three times higher than VanCity expected.

Staff confidence in the small business loan application process was evident in their enthusiastic promotion of the program. In addition to making outbound calls based on marketing leads, staff proactively recommended the loans to existing members and new clients. To put the success into perspective, one branch reported 17 applications during the first two weeks of the pilot; in previous years, 17 in a year would have been considered good.

Follow-up

Due to the program's success, VanCity has decided to introduce a similar pilot for larger business loans. The Small Loan Program continues to be successful, but VanCity is changing its marketing focus to avoid being pigeonholed into the small business niche.

Why it works

The integration with the sales force is a fabulous part of the strategy here. Many marketers make the mistake of not recognizing that the best marketing efforts are wasted if the sales channel does not cooperate. The relationship between banks and small business has typically been strained; using incentives and testimonials meant members of the sales force not only were more receptive to small business, but also sought them out. Staggering the mailing also meant that follow-up from the branch personnel was more likely.

The promise of approval within 24 hours showed an understanding of the time-pressed nature of small business owners, as well as their desire to know the outcome of an application as quickly as possible. In addition, the messaging was very customer-centered; the campaign was designed to express what a small business owner wants ("I want . . ."), rather than to highlight what the bank offers.

Also notable is the positioning of the loans for *businesses* rather than *small businesses.* Many small business owners do not think of their businesses as small; to them, it's just a business.

Another illustration of VanCity's understanding of its market is the frequent use of women in the creative. The Small Loan Program offered loans ranging in value from Can$5,000 to Can$35,000, which means their audience was likely smaller businesses. Women-owned businesses tend to be smaller than the average business (see Chapter 1).

The strategy of running a pilot meant that they were able to anticipate problems in the system before upsetting clients and staff, avoiding further erosion of the relationship between the bank and small business. In addition, creating hype in non-participating branches probably increased sales and awareness.

The letter creative was not particularly unusual in the small business market, but the message itself is what sold. The clear, focused promise is fantastic.

Marketer: NEBS Business Products

Campaign
Thank You For Your Business (see Figure B.12)

We love this campaign for its simplicity. Showing small business owners that their business is appreciated is an underused tactic in this market. In addition, using NEBS' own product line allows the company to showcase its products and give small business owners the opportunity of experiencing first-hand their effectiveness.

Agency
In-house

Background:
While NEBS has an extensive database of small business customers, the average customer uses only one or two products from the NEBS line. Despite receiving regular catalogs featuring their diversified product line, many customers continue to see NEBS as a forms-and-checks provider.

In addition, NEBS traditionally experiences a significant number of one-time purchases. According to Alison Durtnall, director of marketing for NEBS in Canada, only 40 percent of first-time purchasers return within a year.

In the past, NEBS has used telemarketing reps to contact new purchasers, but has met with only limited success in influencing repurchase. They wanted to explore a new way to encourage first-time customers to shorten their purchase cycles and diversify their product orders.

Target

All first time NEBS purchasers from the previous month were included in this test (approximately 2,000 businesses). NEBS specializes in the microbusiness market—the majority of NEBS customers are businesses with one to four employees.

This campaign ran in the Canadian market.

Objectives

- To encourage first-time customers to return to NEBS on a shorter purchase cycle
- To encourage order diversification and increased purchase size by providing gifts at certain purchase levels

Strategy

The strategy was to encourage first-time customers with a reward for new purchases over Can$100.

NEBS is part of the AIR MILES for Business coalition program, a successful loyalty program targeted to small businesses. As a result, they are able to offer AIR MILES reward miles as incentives for customers to make purchases. The base was therefore segmented into two groups: AIR MILES collectors received double reward miles (typically NEBS gives one mile of travel for every Can$10 spent) and noncollectors received a desk clock.

Creative Approach

NEBS used simple thank-you cards with plain envelopes, items that were part of NEBS' own product line (Figure B.12). The copy within was personalized with both the customer's name and details of their previous purchases. The NEBS Vice President signed the cards.

The copy was simple, containing a quick thank-you for the purchase, an explanation of the incentive offer, and a postscript informing the customer that a bestseller catalog was en route.

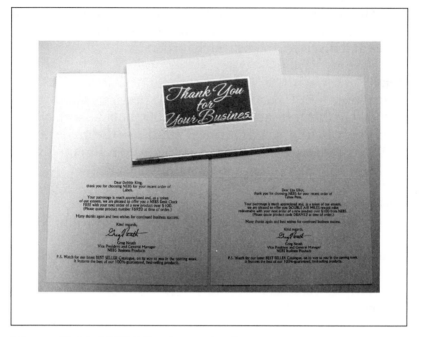

Figure B.12 NEBS Business Products
Source: Courtesy of NEBS Business Products

Contact Method
Direct mail

Cost of Campaign
Although NEBS could not release costs, Durtnall asserted that the cost per sale was much less than with telemarketers or the live sales force.

Results
- Within three weeks, close to 1 percent of the new buyers returned for more products.
- Return purchasers had an average spend 60 percent higher than other buyers.

These results are significant, given that the average NEBS product has to be replaced every eight months and the average buyer buys only one or two products. Durtnall confirms that the quickly growing number of return purchasers likely reflects diversification within the NEBS product line.

Given that the mailing was sent to only 2,000 businesses, NEBS did not test the offers against one another, but may do so in the future.

Follow-up

NEBS is pleased with the results and has continued the campaign over the last few months.

Why it works

Small businesses often tell us that they feel unappreciated by the companies they patronize. This simple "thank-you" strategy goes a long way to recognizing the value of the business that they bring. Because small businesses typically place a high value on service themselves, this customer-centered approach would appeal to them.

The thank-you cards are part of the NEBS product line. Their use in this campaign reinforces the company's belief in its own products: if it is good enough for your business, it is good enough for mine. The folksy, down-home approach of using simple cards was well suited to NEBS customers—typically smaller, established companies that prioritize quality of life over exponential growth of the bottom line. Most NEBS companies are Freedom Fighters or Craftspeople rather than Mountain Climbers.

Because small businesses like value for their money, the offer of an incentive appeals to them. For businesses the size of the NEBS customer, every dollar they spend comes from their own pockets; consequently, something for free appeals to them. Of course, setting a certain purchase level also encourages higher spending.

Like the Royal Bank campaign, this program illustrates that direct mail can be an extremely effective medium for small business. Both of these campaigns found that direct mail compared favorably to telemarketing. Direct mail is a medium that allows the entrepreneur to take in the information on his or her own time, rather than being interrupted during a busy day.

Marketer: American Express

Campaign

American Express™ Corporate Card for Small Business—
Repositioning (see Figure B.13)

Repositioning a product and dealing with a fee increase is a challenge for any marketer. The price-sensitive nature of the small business segment makes this campaign all the more

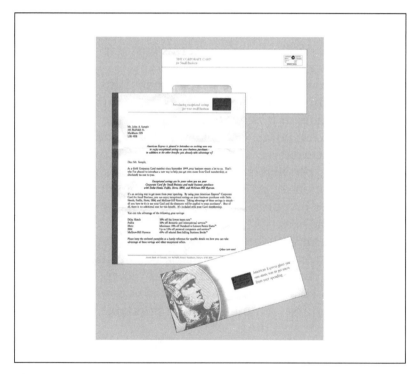

Figure B.13 American Express
Source: Courtesy of American Express

amazing. Through this campaign, American Express succeeded in raising their annual fee by over 50 percent while still increasing spending and membership.

Agency
OgilvyOne Worldwide

Background
American Express has been a long-term player in the SOHO (Small Office, Home Office) market. In the past 18 months, American Express has introduced some significant changes to its Corporate Card for Small Business—changing the color of the plastic to gold, increasing the fee, and adding new benefits. Enhancements to the product included a small business savings program through which entrepreneurs can save up to 45 percent on everyday business purchases with FedEx, IBM, Hertz, Delta Hotels, and McGraw-Hill Ryerson.

However, a key challenge in marketing this revitalized product was to manage a simultaneous fee increase from Can$60 to Can$99 (approximately $40 to $66) annually in order to maintain profitability. In February 1999, statement inserts communicated this fee change. In the following 15 months, all cardholders were billed the increase upon the anniversary of their cards; the billing of a fee is frequently a critical event for customer defection.

This campaign was designed to retain current card members and communicate the value of the card in order to increase charge volume despite the new fee. In addition, the company wanted to continue to acquire new customers to maintain or increase current cards in force.

This campaign ran in the Canadian market, although a similar one was launched in the United States.

Target
- American Express™ Corporate Card for Small Business card members
- Small business owner prospects garnered from partner client lists

The group was predominantly male (71 percent) with an average age of 43.

Objectives

- To maintain the size of the existing franchise (through retention and acquisition) while increasing average spending by 15 percent, thereby increasing profitability through more fee and discount revenue
- To communicate the new annual fee to existing cardholders while highlighting the value of carrying an American Express™ Corporate Card for Small Business.

Strategy

The strategy was to highlight the benefits of the American Express Corporate Card for Small Business in a way that would resonate with small businesses. The savings offered through new partnerships well chosen for the market were the dominant message. This strategy was designed to link the results of proprietary quantitative research—which showed that three of the top-ranked concerns of SOHOs are maintaining good books, finding enough time to do everything, and controlling office overhead costs—to the benefits of the Corporate Card for Small Business (cost savings and expense tracking).

For the existing customer base, the strategy was to send out sequenced direct mail to all cardholders communicating relevant messages in digestible formats. The initial mailing focused on highlighting the new benefits and partnerships to make the fee increase more palatable. Partner mailings followed to enhance impact and increase card spending.

American Express also wanted to increase cards in force by leveraging the client lists of their partners. The company sent a mailing to prospects conveying the message that the American Express Corporate Card for Small Business provides the expense management resources a small business needs. In addition, American Express appealed to the fact that these businesses would save money on purchases that they made anyway.

Highlighting the card's color change to gold was intended to add prestige to the card for both cardholders and prospects. The color change meant that the American Express Corporate Card for Small Business is the only small business credit card in this market that acts as an external indicator of business success.

The campaign began with the communication of the fee increase in February 1999 and continued through much of 2000. It was imperative to continue communicating the key message over the complete year, to ensure that customers were already aware of it when the fee increase was billed.

Creative approach

The target was split into three key segments: Membership Rewards enrollees, nonenrollee cardholders, and prospects. Membership Rewards is the American Express proprietary loyalty program and is an optional benefit on the Corporate Card for Small Business.

The benefit mailing featured a two-page letter introducing the new savings program. For current customers, the tone was appreciative of the clients' business; minor differences appeared in the copy for those in the Membership Rewards program. An included brochure highlighted the details of the benefits. The message was "introducing exceptional savings on your business purchases."

Co-branded partner mailings reinforced the partner-specific savings and benefits.

Contact Method

Direct mail

Cost of Campaign

Although American Express could not release the actual figures, it did indicate that the cost represented 7 percent of the overall Small Business Services budget.

Results

The early returns from this campaign are extremely encouraging. During the first wave of the campaign, despite the fee increase, cards in force increased by 1 percent. In addition, annual average spend per account has increased by 18 percent and net present value has increased by 95 percent. Finally, from April to December 2000, voluntary attrition actually decreased by over 50 percent.

External direct mail acquisition response rates had been eroding steadily over the previous two years because no new product enhancements had been added and competitive pressure had risen. The enhanced value proposition actually increased net response rates by 7 percent despite the fee increase.

Although a fee increase could have potentially had a negative impact on cardholder loyalty, average spend, and acquisition rates, American Express succeeded in communicating to cardholders and prospects that they would be receiving additional value and prestige for the increased annual fee.

Follow-up

The savings program continues to grow and American Express continues to focus on the benefits of the card to its small business client base.

Why it works

American Express's research showed considerable insight into the small business market, recognizing the common concerns around expense management and cost savings. The new product features are completely targeted at small business—not a more general business audience. American Express is well respected in the market as a marketer that understands its small business audience.

The partners American Express has chosen are well targeted. FedEx, Delta Hotels, Hertz, IBM and McGraw-Hill Ryerson are all well respected names —adding to the prestige of the card—and offer products directly targeted to small business. In addition to discounts, the cardholder benefits included memberships to other prestige programs; these included Delta Privilege Blue (which provides expenditure reporting as a benefit) and Hertz #1 Gold (featuring time savings from prefilled forms and less waiting in line).

Establishing these partnerships is a smart strategy for a number of reasons. For the partners, it represents an opportunity to reach a wider audience. In our loyalty program survey, 63 percent of small business owners who could name one or more partner used that partner more after joining a loyalty program.[6]

As for American Express, the strategy now ties the card to incremental services that increase spending. An additional benefit to American Express is access to targeted client lists. Small businesses are very receptive to referrals from trusted partners. Co-branded marketing from their existing suppliers are likely to open doors.

The idea of using a savings program to offset a fee increase is a sound one. According to the Warrillow Report, 52 percent of small business owners that belong to a loyalty program would pay a $50 fee to accelerate their points by 50 percent or increase their discounts by 10 percent.

The creative underscored the prestige of the card by using the card's gold color as a symbol. Respect appeals to most small business owners and carrying the card can act as an outward symbol of success.

In addition, the copy gave the message "your business means a lot to us." This message is one not heard enough by small business owners—especially from their financial service providers. "American Express is one of the best," says Ellen Reid Smith, author of *eLoyalty*. "It is hard to say exactly why this was successful. It is partly due to the offering of savings on things they use today, but fifty percent of it [their success] was due to the empathy that they showed for small business. It is rare that a large company shows such empathy and respect towards smaller ones. This has huge resonance with the small business crowd."

---

6. Warrillow Report, "The Impact of Loyalty Programs on the Buying Behaviors of Small Business Owners," *The Warrillow Report* 04, no. 01.

American Express is used by Amex Bank of Canada under license from American Express Company.

Marketer: Encompass Insurance

Campaign

Brand Launch Campaign (see Figure B.14)

This vertically targeted campaign to independent agents shows a great understanding of what makes the Freedom Fighter segment tick.

Agency

Leo Burnett Agency

Background

Independent insurance agents represent approximately one-third of the personal insurance lines market in the United States and $45 billion in premiums. In late 1999, insurance titan Allstate, who traditionally only sells through Allstate agents, acquired CNA Personal Insurance (a division of CNA Insurance); CNA Personal has existing relationships with 3,700 independent agents, cultivated over 20 years of selling through this channel.

In September 2000, Allstate rebranded their new acquisition as Encompass, a company that would sell exclusively through independent agents. "We have pledged to sell only through independent insurance agents," Ernest A. Lausier, president of Encompass, said at the time of the brand launch. "We help independent agents do what they do best—recommend the coverage that best fits their customers' needs. We want to be the market leader, the carrier of choice among independent agents."

Target

This branding campaign was targeted toward independent insurance agents who sell personal insurance.

A complementary campaign targeted the consumer purchasers.

Objectives

- To position Encompass with independent agents as a small, underdog insurance company
- To create awareness for the company's flagship product, the Universal Insurance Policy—one policy that covers home, auto, vacation, boat, and more with only one application, one bill, and one renewal date

Strategy

In order to create a campaign that resonated with independent agents, Leo Burnett and Encompass did research into this market. Their findings indicated that independent insurance agents place high value on their freedom to choose which insurance is right for their customers. They also value their own independent lifestyle free from the corporate world of the insurance giants.

The strategy was to celebrate this independence with a campaign underscoring the agent's right to choose. The campaign was designed to position Encompass's smaller stature (in terms of market share) as a positive attribute—one that would ensure that they cared more for their customers and would fight for them and the agents that recommended them.

To establish business partner relationships and reach local consumers, Encompass also created a series of co-branded ads with some of their base of independent agent insurers.

Creative approach

"We thought that if we were going to give the agents independence from typical insurance, we should give them independence from typical insurance advertising," said Leo Burnett's creative head.

To underscore the independence theme, Leo Burnett and Encompass created a campaign drawing on the rhetoric and

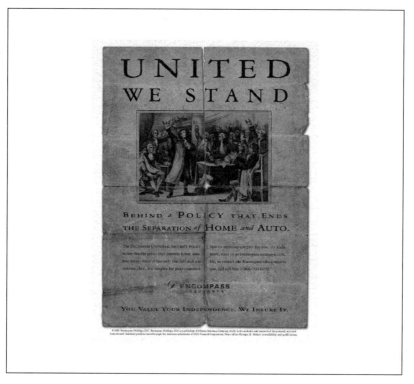

Figure B.14 Encompass Insurance
Source: © Encompass Holdings, LLC

the images of the American Revolution—the war of independence (Figure B.14). Messaging was designed to position Encompass as a smart, spunky underdog willing to fight for the agents who sell its insurance as well as its customers.

The tagline "You value your independence. We insure it." gives the message that by providing quality insurance options, Encompass helps satisfy the independent agent's customers, and will therefore help perpetuate the agent's independent lifestyle.

The look of the print campaign is distinctive: the pages are designed to look like weathered parchment and the images are black and white sketch drawings, the kind that appear in high school history books.

Contact method

Print ads were placed in insurance trade magazines. Co-branded ads (with agents) ran in local market newspapers.

Cost of campaign

Unavailable

Results

Leo Burnett was not able to share results but indicated that Encompass was pleased with the campaign.

Follow-up

In addition to continuing with the print and co-branded advertising, the campaign is expanding to include postcards and direct mail.

Why it works

This campaign is very well targeted to the Freedom Fighter in the insurance sector. Most Freedom Fighters started their own businesses so that they could be their own bosses; this campaign acknowledges that state of mind perfectly and should appeal to this segment. In addition, because the company positioned itself as small, its small business audience will be more likely to identify with it.

The marketing is more effective because Encompass does not sell directly to the consumer; the company is therefore not competing with its own clients, as many players do in the insurance sector. This lack of channel conflict makes the independent agent more likely to trust the company. The co-branded advertising underscores this quality and reinforces the company's partnership with small business. In addition, the creative execution is interesting and a little unusual; it is likely to get noticed.

Index

Index

Index